Silver Burdett Picture Histories

The Days of the Mayas, Aztecs, and Incas

Louis-René Nougier
Illustrated by Pierre Joubert

Library of Congress Cataloging in Publication Data

Nougier, Louis-René, 1912–
    The days of the Mayas, Aztecs, and Incas.

    (Silver Burdett picture histories)
    Translation of: Au temps des Mayas, des Aztèques, et des Incas.
    Includes index.
    Summary: Discusses the work, homes, crafts, customs, religions, and architecture of
the early Indians of North, Central, and South America, from the cold northern regions to
the tropical forests.
        1. Indians—Antiquities—Juvenile literature.
    2. America—Antiquities—Juvenile literature.
    [1. Indians—Antiquities. 2. America—Antiquities]
    I. Joubert, Pierre, 1910–   ill. II. Title.
    III. Series.
    E61.N75513   1985   970.01   85-40208
    ISBN 0-382-09086-1 (pbk.)
    ISBN 0-382-06888-2 (lib. bdg.)

Translated by Francoise Burgess
from *La vie privée des Hommes: Au temps des Mayas, des Aztèques et des Incas*

First published in France in 1981 by
Librairie Hachette, Paris

American adaptation by Nan Buranelli for Silver Burdett Company.

Adapted and published in the United States in 1985 by Silver Burdett Company,
Morristown, N. J.

Contents

AMERICA

The Americas, the New World . . . for five hundred years, now, these new lands have been stirring people's imaginations and haunting their dreams. First, they lured the conquistadors—the warriors of the conquest, then the explorers, and most recently the immigrants from Europe and Asia.

This fascination for America began with Christopher Columbus at the end of the fifteenth century. This land still titillates the imagination of those Europeans, who, despite the discovery of the New World, remain inhabitants of the Old World. America is far away, huge, and full of promise. It stretches from the area of the North Pole to the area of the South Pole. It is a magnet for the poor of undeveloped countries, but also for those Europeans and Asians who dream of new horizons. They follow in the footsteps of many Europeans who, in a time when kings were absolute rulers, came to find gold or spices, or to exploit the Indians.

IMAGES AND ILLUSIONS OF AMERICA

The plains of the Far West, with their huge herds of buffaloes; the fever of the gold rush; the lootings and the massacres of the conquistadors; the legend of "Eldorado," (a name that literally means "the land of gold"); the treasure of the Incas; the mystery of the lost cities of the Andes; the fur traders of the Great North and their wolf hounds; the amazing story of Cortes and his thirteen horsemen whom the Indians mistakenly believed to be Gods because they had never seen horses before; the mysteries of the Mayan temples; the human sacrifices on the platform of Tchac Mol. These are the traditional images of a far off America that meld and blend in people's minds, often with little regard for chronology or historical accuracy. They are a ready combination of fantasy, which is not always based in truth, and legend, which sometimes is.

CHRISTOPHER COLUMBUS

All these tall tales, stories of adventure, images and illusions, stem from one source—Christopher Columbus, discoverer of the New World. True or false, they are deeply rooted in the national memory of each country, a memory shaped by the tremendous upheaval caused by the formation of the modern western states at the end of the Middle Ages.

In 1492, as everyone knows, Christopher Columbus, the Genoese navigator, was, at long last, within sight of his goal. All the energy he had expended in pleading with Europe's kings and wealthy patrons to help him fulfill his dream was about to be rewarded. Westward he steered with his three caravels, financed by the Spanish sovereigns, Isabella of Castile and Ferdinand of Aragon. If he succeeded, all the riches of the "Indies" would be theirs.

On the morning of October 12, Columbus achieved his goal. He raised the flag of Castile on the beach of the first island he reached. This island, called *Guanahani* by the native people, is now known as Watling Island, one of the Bahamas, off the coast of North America. The year 1492 was indeed a turning point in history.

The new land rapidly revealed its vast wealth. It was populated by many "Indians" (this was the name given to the local population by Columbus because he thought he had found the East Indies). How were these Indians living in 1492 when they were discovered? Christopher Columbus and his men looked upon them as sadly different from themselves. They thought the Indian led a miserable life and was a mere "savage." This derogatory term would be used as a way of justifying all the plundering, conquests, and massacres the

Europeans would perpetrate. Yet the Indians had a distinctive culture of their own, with an economy and specific traditions reflecting their environment on this continent. But the Spaniards did not come to this land to get to know or understand them. They were in the Americas to claim land and riches in the name of the Christian monarchs of Spain. They exploited the Indians and at the same time tried to convert them to their Christian faith. The result was devastating to these native Americans.

THE TRUE DISCOVERERS OF AMERICA AND THE BERING "BRIDGE"

The true discoverers of America did not come from the sea, but over land. As hunters of mammoths, they probably started off from the taiga and the tundra in the northern parts of Europe and Asia. (The forest that covers this area is called the taiga, and the steppe covered with moss and lichen is the tundra.) They were contemporary with the prehistoric reindeer-hunters of Europe, and ancestors of the artists of Rouffignac, of about 12,000 B.C., who were to carve and draw more than 150 mammoths in the caves of Perigord in southwestern France.

The hunters who lived farthest north are the true discoverers of America—they were its first inhabitants and populated the New World. Today, fifty miles of sea separate the cape that lies on the eastern edge of Asia from Cape Prince of Wales in the extreme northwest of America. (Since early times, the great straits of our world have aroused people's desire to cross them, more often than they have discouraged them from doing so.) On a clear day, the snow-capped mountains of Alaska are visible from Asia. This means that one can cross the sea between Asia and America without losing sight of land for one moment.

In ancient times hunters chased mammoths across what is now the Bering Strait without getting their feet wet—because there was no such strait. The weather then was extremely cold and much of the liquid mass of the oceans had been frozen into ice. This ice covered the tops of mountains and spread over the northern part of the continent. The shores of the oceans therefore retreated sixty feet, leaving the strait, which was only twenty-three feet deep, high and dry.

What is now the strait once again stretched like a broad bridge between the Asian and American continents. It had become an isthmus and people crossed it without realizing it was one. Thus, hunters of buffalo, reindeer, and mammoths, crossed the bridge without

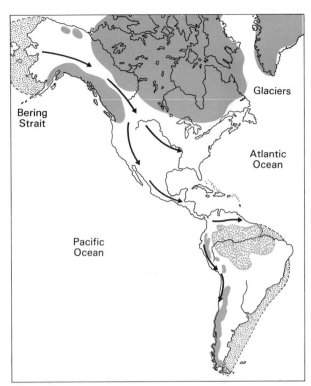

The path followed by the prehistoric hunters, who crossed the Bering Strait. The Northern glaciers and the equatorial forest were the two main natural obstacles to human settlements.

Tenochtitlan, the Aztec capital

In 1476, the Aztec capital of Tenochtitlan annexed the large commercial center of Tlatelolco, a market town of 25,000 to 30,000 people. As a result, more than 500,000 people lived on a mere 2,000 acres in Tenochtitlan. By comparison, at the end of the eighteenth century, more than 500,000 people lived in Paris, the capital of France, on 15,600 acres.

A codex showing the cult of Chimecoalt, the Aztec goddess of corn.

knowing that they were leaving Asia behind. They had become the first explorers to set foot on American land. The way was clear, the country uninhabited, a paradise for hunters, who love vast expanses and little competition.

This migration from Asia to America probably took place between 30,000 and 10,000 B.C. By 7000 B.C. the hunters had explored and populated all of their new home, right down to the southernmost tip of the continent at Tierra del Fuego.

PRIMITIVE LIFE

These early American pioneers of the late prehistoric era led the same kinds of lives as their contemporaries in Europe, Asia, and Africa. Until 10,000 B.C., all human beings enjoyed much the same type of existence. So that when a discovery was made, such as that of the needle, it spread across the world quickly, that is to say within a few thousand years.

In about 10,000 B.C. the climate grew milder. The ice melted. The water level of the oceans rose again and flooded the Bering "bridge." Only a few mountain tops remained above sea level. The American continent was permanently cut off from Asia, its only source of human beings. From then on, America had to use its own resources to survive. However, the immigrant hunter populations were large enough to grow rapidly and to develop ways of overcoming the periodic hunger crises that punctuate the history of humankind.

From the Atlantic to the Pacific, the Americans solved their own problems. They fought wild animals—and the jaguar became the fearsome symbol of the struggle. They mastered nature itself. They irrigated the dry lands of Mexico and drained the swamps of Texcoco, where Mexico City stands today. In the Andes they invented terrace cultivation, and built low stone walls to support the terraces. To feed themselves, they discovered and improved the qualities of a native grain called corn. With the passing centuries, the corn cob would grow to six times its original size.

These efforts were limited by the natural resources of the continent. The Indians never knew the horse, which had disappeared thousands of years before. They did not raise cattle because there were no animals to domesticate, except for turkeys. Even though they had discovered the concept of a circle, they did not know of the wheel, and so they had no carts or wagons. People walked on the hard Inca roads, carrying heavy loads on their backs, and using the Andean llamas only to carry ingots. Last, but not least, they knew nothing of iron or bronze and they hammered gold and copper in much the same way as they would stones.

No cattle, no iron, no wheel! Nevertheless, the Indians became skilled artisans. They wove the fibers of the maguey, a native cactus. They invented richly colored geometric designs. They were builders who cut stones with mortises and joined column shafts with tenons. They built huge cities to meticulously ordered plans. They invented games and were the first people to use heavy rubber balls. They erected high pyramids, topped by temples where the blood of human sacrifices sometimes flowed. Priests celebrated the ancient worship of the old fire god and later, of the jaguar, a cult directly linked to the hunt. With the cultivation of corn they introduced the rain god, the fearsome Tlaloc. Corn itself later became a god. The Mayan priests were expert mathematicians and astronomers. They engraved hieroglyphs that to this day still remain undeciphered.

MARITIME INFLUENCES

This isolated continent was rarely touched by intrusion from the sea. Asian hunters crossed the Bering Strait in kayaks made of hides and, hopping from island to island, reached Alaska. Canoes from the Aleutian Islands would follow the same route. Later, daring sailors, carried by the winds and the currents, would cross the Pacific Ocean. They brought Japanese pottery techniques to Ecuador and Peru. From Europe, in the sixth century, St. Brendan the Irish monk is said to have reached Newfoundland, on a frail bark made of thirty-two oxen hides sewn together. In 1976–77 Tim Severin repeated this feat.

In 981, four hundred years after St. Brendan, Erik the Red followed the same northern route from Norway to Iceland, and from Iceland to Greenland. In the year 1000 his son, Lief Eriksson, reached the coast of North America. For the first time, the Vikings found themselves face to face with the American Indians, the *Skraelings*, or savages as they perceived them. The representatives of the two civilizations clashed violently. Armed with spears and arrows and equipped with light canoes, the Indians fought off the Vikings. There were too few Vikings and their arms were too similar to those of the Indians; they were doomed to fail. They could neither dominate the Indians nor settle this new land to prepare the way for more immigrants.

In 1492, Christopher Columbus landed in the New World. He had gunpowder. From then on, firearms would talk, argue, and convince.

The animals of the time

Animals that have disappeared
- *the mammoth, around 10,000 B.C.*

Animals on the way to extinction
- *the caribou: it still survives in the Great North*
- *the seal and the whale*
- *the various types of camel*
  - *the guanaco, the oldest of them all**
  - *the llama, which carries heavy loads*
  - *the vicuna, with thick, warm fur**
  - *the alpaca, whose wool is in great demand*
- *the nadou, a type of ostrich*

Animals indigenous to the American continent
- *the buffalo (American bison)*
- *the guinea pig, imported from Peru*
- *the musk duck*
- *the ocellated Yucatan turkey*

*The guanaco and vicuna have remained wild.

J. BOTTIN

A figurine of a wolf

7

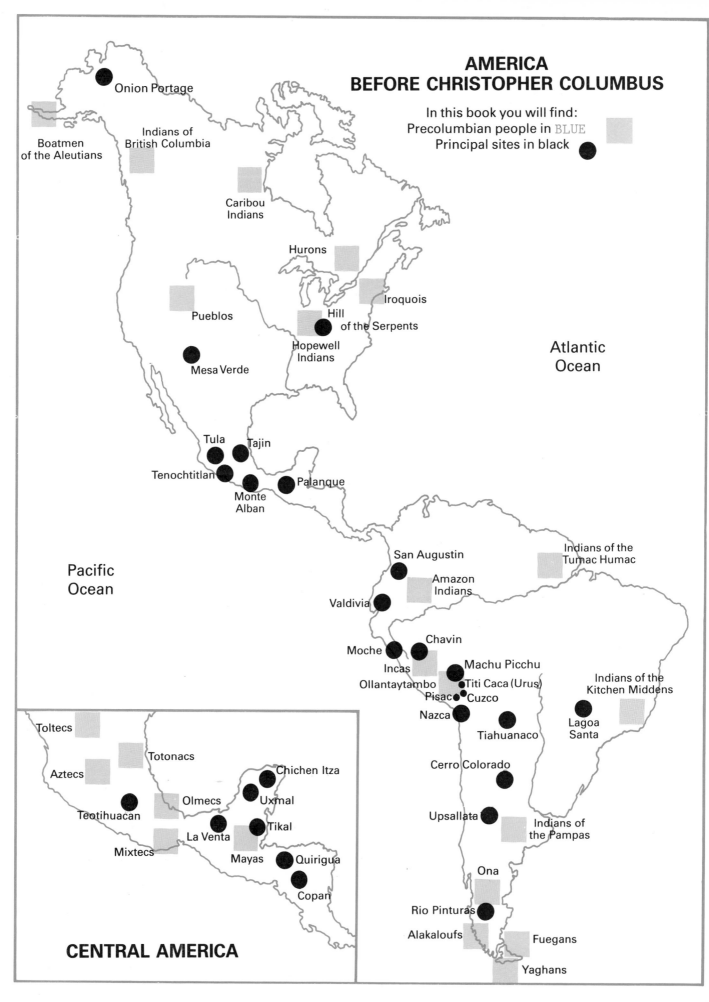

AMERICA
BEFORE CHRISTOPHER COLUMBUS

In this book you will find:
Precolumbian people in BLUE
Principal sites in black

Onion Portage

Boatmen
of the Aleutians

Indians of
British Columbia

Caribou
Indians

Hurons

Iroquois

Pueblos

Hill
of the Serpents

Hopewell
Indians

Mesa Verde

Atlantic
Ocean

Pacific
Ocean

Tula

Tajin

Tenochtitlan

Palanque

Monte
Alban

San Augustin

Indians of the
Tumac Humac

Amazon
Indians

Valdivia

Chavin

Moche

Machu Picchu

Incas

Ollantaytambo

Titi Caca (Urus)

Indians of the
Kitchen Middens

Pisac

Cuzco

Nazca

Lagoa
Santa

Tiahuanaco

Cerro Colorado

Upsallata

Indians of
the Pampas

Ona

Rio Pinturas

Alakaloufs

Fuegans

Yaghans

CENTRAL AMERICA

Toltecs

Totonacs

Aztecs

Chichen Itza

Teotihuacan

Olmecs

Uxmal

La Venta

Tikal

Mixtecs

Mayas

Quirigua

Copan

The First Americans

The human species probably began some three million years ago. Our ancestors, however, (pithecanthropus and sinanthropus) go much further back in time—some ten, fifteen, maybe even twenty million years. Scholars are still hoping to discover the fundamental secret of our origins. So far, our oldest ancestors have been found in Africa, notably in East Africa. However, recent discoveries have unearthed fossils in the north of India and in places in China that support the theory of the Asian origin of humanity, presumably in central Asia in the Siwalick mountains, a range that runs parallel to the Himalayas.

We know definitely that human beings did not appear first in America. There was no trace of them on this huge continent as recently as 30,000 years ago. So, Asia is probably the cradle of the human race and certainly the starting place for its rapid expansion throughout the world. The successive waves of migrations that populated America all came from Asia. They began 30,000 years ago and continued over a period of 20,000 years.

During the last Ice Age, Asia and North America were linked by a natural causeway, an isthmus more than 600 miles wide. The glaciers of the North and South Poles and the mountains expanded over a much larger area than before, forcing the sea level to drop by more than 200 feet. New lands emerged, and what is now the Bering Strait became a large strip of land that humans and animals began to use, though quite unaware that they were crossing a true natural bridge.

And so, quite naturally, the first Americans were hunters on land. With their assagais, or their sharp obsidian and silex-headed spears, they chased the game whose meat they needed to survive. They crossed the vast expanses of Siberia and reached the American continent to the east.

Some of the animals that had preceded them have since disappeared. The mammoths never got beyond the high plateaus of Mexico and disappeared about 10,000 B.C. An early type of horse disappeared at the same time (the horse we know was brought to America by the Spaniards).

o the left (i.e., to the West), are the last mountains of Asia continu-
g the Kamtchatka range, and to the right (i.e., to the East) the first
eaks of America—Alaska and the Rocky Mountains. Harried by dar-

ing hunters, mammoths trudge over the Bering bridge. Together,
they leave Asia and come to America over dry land. This happened
between 30,000 and 10,000 B.C.

berian mammoths showed the way to America. Here they have
en ensnared in the lagoons of Lake Texcoco (near present-day
exico City) where hunters killed them with obsidian spearheads.
ese hunters have erected temporary campsites for shelter.

On the coast of the gulf of Veracruz, the tropical forest reigns supreme. Vines make it almost impenetrable. It was the home of the
jaguar, who replaced the old fire god, born of the volcanoes, and became the god of the Olmecs. Here hunters are fighting a jaguar.

unting was the way of life of the first inhabitants of the Americas
r the 10,000 years that preceded our era. When these hunters left
ia their techniques did not change but the available game did. On
e high plateaus of Patagonia, the southernmost tip of America,

these men, armed with bows and obsidian-headed spears, track
down a wild relative of the camel, the guanaco. Red and black paint-
ings of such hunting scenes still cover cave walls. They are similar to
stag hunting scenes which appear in Spanish caves.

Boatmen and Sailors

For a long time the hunters trying to penetrate the interior of this new continent used the natural paths provided by the terrain. They followed the often unfriendly coastlines and, more particularly, traveled along the high plateaus running north to south along the Rocky Mountain chain. From the Rockies they ventured into the Mexican highlands, and then the Andes. At last they reached Cape Horn.

In about 10,000 B.C., the tongue of land known as the Isthmus of Bering disappeared. From then on a strait separated the two continents. So the second wave of settlers came from the sea. It didn't take long, as the sounds spread wider and wider, for the immigrants to grow used to crossing them by sea. A maritime tradition was born.

The Arctic is a frozen, barren region with no trees. So the people inhabiting this area had no wood to build boats with. The first hunters learned to sew the hides of animals together. This is why their boats were made from hides.

The skin coracles seen today on the Aran islands, off the east coast of Ireland, are strange survivals of these ancient models. They give credibility to the story of St. Brendan dating from the sixth century.

Coming from Japan, sometimes by way of the Aleutian Islands, sometimes more directly, boatmen crossed the North Pacific. They stuck closely to the coast, content at first to establish fishing villages there. But the cold, foggy weather along the water soon persuaded them to move to the high plateaus. There they settled and learned to cultivate the land.

Thorfin Karlsefni, an audacious Viking chief landed in Vinland, the Land of Wine, around the year 1000, on the coast of what is now Maine. The country was rich in salmon and green pastures. Wild vines grew riotously. But Thorfin Karlsefni's attempt to settle in America, although more historical than St. Brendan's, failed. America had to wait for Christopher Columbus.

The Vikings meet the *Skraelings*, the American "savages."

12

shed relentlessly by new waves of immigrants, the Alakoloufs and Yahgans finally reached Tierra del Fuego, which is at the south-most tip of America. They lived by collecting seafood, in a cold mate on a land ceaselessly swept by storms and wind.

These people followed the cold Humboldt current coming down from the South Pole along the Andean coast. This small boat is relatively stable thanks to two small empty hulls, secured on each side, that give it balance.

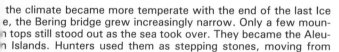

Irish tale of the sixth century relates the miraculous voyage of St. ndan. He left the east coast of Ireland in a coracle, a boat made m thirty-two oxen hides, sewn together and secured on a wicker me, to reach America by way of Iceland and Greenland.

the climate became more temperate with the end of the last Ice e, the Bering bridge grew increasingly narrow. Only a few moun-n tops still stood out as the sea took over. They became the Aleu-n Islands. Hunters used them as stepping stones, moving from

Small fishing villages began to pop up beside the sea and in the nar-row litoral plains that were dominated by the first foothills of the An-des. These first inhabitants of Peru left the sea fogs behind and climbed into the deep valleys which ran inland to colonize the highlands.

island to island, to reach America. They couldn't carve their boats out of tree trunks since there were no big trees around. So their boats had light frames, made of bones or branches , and were covered with animal hides.

Skilled Hunters and Fishermen

A carefully planned economy is often based on hunting an animal whose every part can be used. Such was the case in the "civilization of the buffalo." Every part of the animal was usable. You ate its flesh. You strung your bows with its nerves and sinews. You used its horns as receptacles and its bones to make tools, borers, or awls. You dug the ground with its shoulder blade and you burned its fat in your lamps to see at night. Even its dung was not wasted. It was dried and burned to provide heat.

The Indians of the temperate plains of the Far West lived for a long time by exploiting the buffalo. Unfortunately, both Indians and buffaloes who depended on each other for survival were stupidly and pitilessly massacred in the nineteenth century. It is a page of history that is hard to forget.

For survival in the colder regions of the north, other American civilizations depended on hunting the great stag, the wapiti, the reindeer, and the caribou. A few thousand years before, the same types of hunting civilizations had existed in prehistoric Europe.

The sea, always more hospitable to humans and animals than the land, sustained over a longer period such economies based on the exploitation of animals—for instance, those depending on the whale and the seal in the icy Arctic wastes. For awhile, the salmon was the source of a thriving economy. The salmon migrates at regular and predictable intervals, and its flesh, when dried, could be stored and eaten during the non-fishing season.

The huge, dense equatorial forest that stretches from the Tropic of Cancer to the Tropic of Capricorn offered meager and uncertain opportunities for either hunting or fishing. Furthermore, its inaccessibility made human settlement extremely difficult. The few who attempted it led isolated lives, cut off from the outside world.

Fishermen paddle their beechbark canoes in the Straits of Magellan, between the high cliffs of Patagonia and Tierra del Fuego. These Yahgans hunted sea otters with spears and slings.

...e, an Amazonian hunter uses a ten-foot blowgun, made from a ...ow bamboo stick, to blow deadly poisonous arrows. This poison, ...wn as curare, kills instantly. The hunter carries it in the small pot ...ging around his neck.

...e trunks of six balsas would provide enough boards to build this ...t. The balsa tree has very light wood and floats like cork. These ...azonian Indians are going down the Madre de Dios, a river that ...es in the Bolivian highlands.

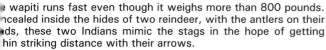

...e wapiti runs fast even though it weighs more than 800 pounds. ...ncealed inside the hides of two reindeer, with the antlers on their ...ds, these two Indians mimic the stags in the hope of getting ...hin striking distance with their arrows.

The Eskimos who lived in the Great North hunted seals and whales. They half buried their huts in the ground and supported the roofs with whale ribs. They went sea fishing in the *oumiak*, a hide-covered boat that was indispensable to their survival.

These Indians have created a barrier of nettle fiber nets across some rapids, reinforced by long lines with almost a hundred fishhooks. In the fall, when the salmon go up the river, the Indians have a truly miraculous catch of fish.

Farmers at Work

Each continent might be characterized by a cereal Europe has wheat, Africa has sorghum, Asia ha rice, and America has corn. As agricultural work ers gradually began to till the land instead of merel picking the grains, they made a god of corn. Th corn god was accompanied by Tlaloc, the rain goc for rain is essential to its growth as a plant. To gether with the old fire god and the jaguar god, rep resenting the natural powers of the volcanoes an the animal world of the hunters, they became sym bols of Indian life.

Corn and America have been linked togethe ever since the dawn of the pre-Columbian era. Th oldest wild corn on record dates back to about 700 B.C. It was a scraggy-looking plant of the steppes bearing no more than a dozen tiny grains. The dr climate of the Tehuacan valley fostered its growth Since then rigorous selection has allowed farmer to produce today's heavy ears, corn that yields 20 times more grain than its earlier form did. Nowa days, there are over 1,500 varieties of corn.

Such results have been made possible thank to irrigation. For thousands of years, canals hav brought water to the Tehuacan valley. This suc cessful experiment with corn is probably as old a the cultivation of wheat in Egypt. Indians repeate it with other wild plants such as beans (''frijoles'') pumpkins, calabashes, tomatoes, peppers, and co ton. Between 3000 and 2000 B.C., forty time more people are thought to have lived in the valle than did in 7000 B.C. At the beginning of our era the population was estimated as being about 15 times larger than its original size. If France's pre historic population had grown at the same speed, i would have reached 75 million at the time of th Roman Empire, instead of the 7 million it actuall did.

Even though such figures are hypothetical they provide a clue to understanding the prodigiou development of the Precolombian civilizations tha was to be so brutally interrupted by the Spaniards

The Pisac ''andennes''—or terraces—dominate the deep valle of the Urubamba River which, farther on, flows past the foot Machu Picchu. The Incas tilled the soil of these irrigated terrace with hoes and stone axes (this was the neolithic age). The grew a white corn the quality of which is still unequalled today

The Tehuacan valley, north of Puebla, peasants dig ditches to irrigate the young corn. The presence of candelabra-shaped cactuses indicates a dry soil. Shelters, such as those visible in the background, had been used by farmers since 8000 B.C.

The Texcoco swamps were crisscrossed by canals bordering rectangles of raised ground where people grew flowers and vegetables. These are called *chinampas*. In the native language, Nahuatl, they were given the name of *xochimilco* which means "place of fields and flowers."

The Bolivian altiplano is 9,000 to 12,000 feet high, and is surrounded by the Andean glaciers. Here two guanacos are teamed to draw a swing-plow, while two women dry the leaves of six-foot coca bushes that the men have gathered.

In an Amazon forest clearing, gutted by fire, women collect the swollen roots of cassava between the half-calcified stumps of the trees. They fill big esparto grass baskets, carried by the men, who use a headband strap to support them.

This is a typical Indian village of the Western plains. The tents (tepees) are made of thirteen poles bound together at the top and covered with carefully sewn skins. Wapitis, whose huge antlers are painted in red, decorate the tepee on the left. Women gather the fruit of the mountain ash. When fermented, it will produce an alcoholic beverage. Other women tend to the large leaves of young tobacco plants: when they have been dried they will feed the peace pipe, a long-stemmed pipe that only the village chief is entitled to smoke.

The Lake People

Lakes, as well as seashores, are magnets that draw people searching for a place that offers a combination of these two invaluable natural resources: water and land. Such a combination has always facilitated the organization of social life, and has often explained why new civilizations developed where they did.

The Urus, of Lake Titicaca located 12,000 feet high in the heart of the Andes, are undoubtedly the descendants of the first immigrants who entered this continent across the Bering Strait. At the beginning of the twentieth century, they themselves declared: "We, people of the lake, are not men." They believed they had come before men and even before the sun. But late arrivals, it seems, the Aymaras, had chased them from the shore and literally pushed them out onto the lake. Thus the Urus could rely only on the resources offered by the water. A reed, the totora, became their staple food: they boiled or roasted the rhizomes of the totora to make them edible. They ground them to make a flour that they mixed with water and ate.

The Urus also liked to suck the rhizomes' sweet marrow and to make a fermented drink from it. Lake fish, eggs that were gathered from the nests of water birds (much as the Tierra del Fuego people did), and a few birds that they hunted, complemented this diet.

The totora being the only raw material available they built huts with it and made mats (their only furniture). Most important, they built those long boats s typical of their culture, with up-turned ends, made o bundles of reeds tightly packed together to make th boat waterproof. These boats are identical to one found on the lakes and swamps of Argentina and alon the Peruvian coast. They are also found on Easter Is land, on the shores of Lake Chad, and on the marshe and banks of the Nile where people used papyrus in stead of totora. Some years ago the navigator Tho Heyerdahl succeeded in crossing the Atlantic on tw boats made with braided papyrus bundles. He calle them Ra I and Ra II.

Bamboo was the true wealth of the Urus. The totora in bundles, dry ing in front of their huts, was used to build boats.

The all-purpose plant of the Urus, the totora, grew in the shallow waters of Lake Titicaca. The Urus used this straight but pliable reed for their ship-building activities: once cut and bundled, the reeds were packed in long rolls which were then tightly bound together and shaped into a boat with distinctive up-turned ends.

...e tip of Tierra del Fuego, thousands of seabirds shelter in the ...ks of the high cliffs of Cape Horn. The Fuegians came here in ... frail and narrow boats and climbed the dangerous cliffs to steal ...irds' eggs from their nests.

...e than a mile above sea level, on the high plateau of Mexico, Lake ...cuaro harbored an interesting tribe of mountain fishermen. In ... boats they head for the shores of the lake's islands. They are ...g huge hoop nets equipped with two pockets and two openings

A flat-bottomed reed raft moves slowly on the waters of Lake Titicaca. A soft breeze blows in its three square sails also made of reeds. Small, stone replicas of similar boats have been found on Easter Island, in the middle of the Pacific, 2,000 miles away from the Andes.

and lashed to a long pole. When the fisherman hauls up his net, it looks like the wings of a huge butterfly. In the setting sun the nets quiver with masses of pearly fishes, the *pecito blanco*, a succulent fish.

Homes in the Lowlan
and the Highlands

Every group of people builds their homes accordir
to the region and their way of life. The materia
they use depend on the natural resources availab
in the area. On a continent that stretches fro
Alaska and Baffin Island, home of the ice floe, a
the way down to the cold regions of Tierra d
Fuego and Cape Horn, swept by rain, winds, ar
storms, there was a considerable and quite surpri
ing diversity of both natural resources and home

In the north, there was the log cabin, built f
protection from the cold and heavy snowfalls. The
there was the conical tent of the roaming hunt
who just threw buffalo hides over a few poles l
had hastily put together. In drier climates, hous
were made of sun-baked clay bricks or of larg
stones, depending on the nature of the soil. In Ce
tral America, the climate is hot, heavy and humi
and thick tropical forests cover the area. Therefor
the Mayas built their huts upon earthen platform
raised above the marshes to avoid tropical fever
The light reed frame of these houses served a dou
ble purpose—the wind blew easily through i
bringing the much sought-after relief of cool ai
and it also withstood the shocks of frequent eartl
quakes in ways that heavy structures could not. I
contrast, an Inca temple planted its massive stor
foundations solidly in the ground. The hut could b
rebuilt rapidly while the temple was intended to la
forever. On the 10,000-foot-high altiplano, the Bo
livian and Peruvian high plateaus, houses wei
half-buried in the ground to withstand cold, wind
weather, while the fishermen of Lake Titicaca sca
tered their dwellings along its shores and on i
moving islands of reeds.

This very young American continent di:
played a greater variety of housing styles than th
Old World had produced during its million years o
existence. The pre-Columbians, who had to ada
to an extraordinary diversity of landscapes and cl
mates, economies and ways of life, demonstrate
remarkable qualities of inventiveness that the co
quistadors were to stifle and destroy forever.

The breathtaking chalk canyons of the Mesa Verde are locate
in Colorado. The Pueblo Indians built the clay and stone hous
of their village one on top of the other, beneath the enormo
overhang of the protective cliffs.

...atagonia a lean-to sheltered these Alakaloufs. They lived naked ...rubbed their bodies with whale fat to protect them against the ... When Western civilization reached them, they began to wear ...hes. They let these clothes dry on their bodies when they were ... As a result the Alakaloufs were killed off by tuberculosis.

...imos hunted and fished on Baffin Island. They built hemispheric ...os: large bricks of frozen snow were hacked out with a knife, ...n assembled and cemented with fresh snow which, when it ...ted, sealed the cracks.

...he Yucatan forests, corn was grown in clearings. The Mayas built ...r huts with loosely bound reeds to let the breezes circulate. That-...d palm leaves, used for the roofs, offered protection against ...vy rains. Furniture consisted of a few hammocks.

These squat houses are built with logs or roughly hewn planks. They stand in a clearing, surrounded by tall Douglas firs, in British Columbia. The slant of the two-sided roof is because of the winter's rains and snow falls. The totem poles may reach a height of sixty feet.

Teotihuacan, ''City of the Gods,'' displayed a pattern of harmonious squares. This house, located at the base of the Pyramid of the Sun, is typical of the architecture of the city. Its square rooms open on a patio-market. Stairways lead to the terraces and the upper level.

Cooking

Corn appeared first in the Tehuacan area, north of Puebla, in Mexico. The cobs were small and few in number. But, thanks to irrigation, they gradually grew larger and more plentiful. Eventually, corn spread along the Pacific Coast—to the north as far as California and to the south along the whole area of the Andes as far as Patagonia at the tip of the hemisphere. These were the lines followed by the early migrations, and great urban civilizations were to grow up along them.

The staple grain of America, corn was eaten in many different ways. People munched it raw. When roasted on a white-hot stone, it was a delicacy. When the grains had been soaked in limewater they were ground in corn-grinding vessels called *metates* to make a handkneaded dough which was then shaped into flat pancakes and baked. This pancake is still a staple food of Americans, from the Rio Grande, on the United States border, to the tip of the southern penisula. The pancakes were filled with ground meat, mashed beans, crushed peppers, or fish fillets. A variety of soils and climates also provided a wide assortment of fruits and vegetables, including papayas, mangos, guavas, citrus fruits, bananas, coconuts, and even the fruit of the nopal, a kind of cactus.

The maguey, the agave cactus of the desert, grows very slowly. It blossoms only when it is ten years old, and then dies. Its yellow flower, at the end of a long stem several feet high, is a common sight in the Mexican landscape. The maguey is an all-purpose fruit. A liquid stored in its base quenched the thirst of Indians crossing the desert. Cultivated in quantity it provided up to five hundred quarts of juice which, when fermented, became *pulque*, a powerful alcoholic beverage. In Aztec society only people past the supposedly-wise age of 70 were allowed to drink it freely.

Once the corn had been cut with an obsidian sickle, the cobs were picked off the stems, gathered in baskets, then dried on grids. The harvesting of corn, the first staple food to become a god, was an occasion for great celebration.

e are some very sophisticated culinary instruments! Shaped as ders and crushers, the *metates* were hewn out of the volcanic alt of Popocatepetl. Corn was ground on the rectangular metate. en and red peppers were crushed in the circular one.

Colorful friezes decorated the long entrance hall of a Mitla house. Geometric patterns were predominant, reminiscent of the Greek key pattern. A young Mixtec girl is crushing *frijoles* (beans). She will add peppers to the otherwise bland mash to sharpen its taste.

tifling, exuberant forest covers the steep slopes of the mountains the Tehuantepec peninsula, in the heart of Central America. Its onut trees, with their long, quivering palms, grow right to the e of the sea in the Gulf of Veracruz. The palms were used to make

light, airy canopies that provided shelter from the harsh rays of the sun. What a delight it was to taste the fresh milk of the coconut, split by a thick obsidian blade, and then eat its white, sweet smelling meat. Nearby the green waters of the gulf sprayed the air with salt.

maguey was a blessing for the Indians. Several quarts of a ch-appreciated, if sickly sweet liquid are stored in its base. The Ins sucked it through reed straws into a gourd. The liquid was then ed in a skin jar or a pot and left to ferment and become *pulque*.

How expectantly these young children wait for a feast. Their mother is cooking the golden corn dough on hot stones that will transform it into crunchy, savory pancakes. These were the staple food of Precolombian people. More heated stones are waiting on the open fire.

Pottery Making in Tlatilco

The shallow banks of Lake Texcoco have always attracted human settlements. The first signs of human activity appeared about 2400 B.C. when hunters built a platform on which to camp, standing free of the pebbly beach. The tools they used were made of andesite, a volcanic rock which is difficult to shape. Between 1500 and 1000 B.C. peasant farmers replaced hunters. They settled around the lake at Ticoman, Zacatenco, and Tlatilco, and built reed huts. Tlatilco provided a good supply of water, top-quality clay and, for a few centuries, enough wood to heat ovens. This is why it became a great pottery center. Artisans shaped large vessels by hand, designed to hold water or *pulque* (made of agave sap), earthen silos to preserve peppers and corn, smaller vessels for making soup, still smaller ones for hot sauces, and tiny ones for exotic perfumes.

They also created innumerable small figurines, mostly delicate nude female bodies. Today, we find these statuettes in tombs, buried with the dead, underneath houses, or in large cemeteries. Household rubbish, including figurines that had been broken or damaged as they were being made, has accumulated in huge garbage pits, over twenty-five feet deep.

At the beginning of our era the figurines began to change. Males appeared more often. Scenes were made depicting couples, or a mother and child. Some artists sculpted large single heads, dancers, acrobats, double-headed monsters, or maimed and sick creatures, done so realistically that we can diagnose the nature of their diseases today. Enormous faces with bulging cheeks led the way to the monumental heads later sculpted by the Olmecs, the mother civilization of America.

Sometime around the year 1000 B.C. many ceramic studios were grouped in the village of Tlatilco. They produced an abundant variety of objects such as cooking vessels and countless small lively figurines made to be buried in tombs.

A Peruvian pottery maker is wearing many necklaces. She puts finishing touches on a mochica figurine representing a warrior [that] has been decorated with brightly colored geometric designs. [Eve]n though these patterns are similar to the Greek key pattern the [rese]mblance is pure coincidence.

The people living on the altiplano near the Inca capital of Cuzco have been making the same type of adobe for centuries. These clay bricks are shaped in molds made of narrow boards, dried in the sun, and then used to build houses.

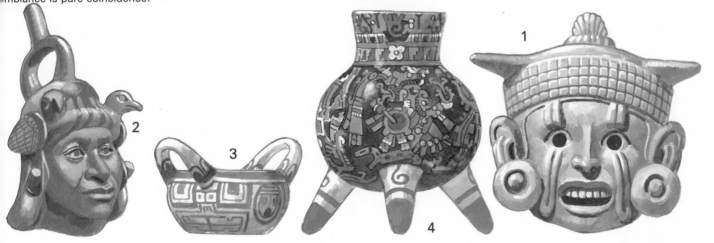

[An]dean ceramics have always displayed a considerable richness of [for]m and decoration. The different styles of the pieces (shavin, mo-[chi]ca, nasca, chimu) allow us to date them accurately. The shapes [are] varied—jars or domestic receptacles, vessels in the form of [ma]sks (1), or of human faces (2), some of them so well done that they look like true portraits. There is variety too in the handles (3), the feet (tripod vessel (4),) and in the astonishing richness of the polychrome decoration of the nasca vessels (4). The handled vessel called a *stirrup* (2) is a realistic portrait from the mochica period.

[In] the Argentinian pampas, one Indian coats a huge jar made of [tigh]tly braided fibers with wild beeswax, to make it waterproof. The [oth]er Indian decorates the vessel by pressing thin cords around it in [the] wax matrix.

In this typical New Mexican village, near the Rio Grande, stone and adobe houses are huddled together around the base of a cliff. A Pueblo Indian, who belongs to the civilization called the basketmakers, weaves a large bell-shaped basket.

With Fire, Ax, and Hoe

Pre-Columbian life in general was based on farming and hunting. Like all primitive societies, this one respected nature and did not seek to change it. Food production was based on crops, since domesticated cattle were unknown in the Americas. In order to produce beans, calabashes, corn, and yams, the early farmers had to literally create fields with soil good enough for farming. They used fire, axes, and hoes to clear patches out of the dense forest, and they built terraces to tame the steep slopes of the Andes. Their methods of land development differed according to the varying climates produced by the unique topography of America.

In some areas, the soil had to be drained of its excess water. Thus, in the heart of the Mexican high plateaus, canals were dug out of the lagoons of Lake Texcoco, on whose banks native Americans have lived for more than 2,000 years. The Mayas also dug canals in the forests of Peten, where the heavy and endless rains frequently turned the land into vast swamps.

These canals required constant upkeep, and failure to maintain them was one reason for the collapse of the Mayan civilization.

In other areas, however, water had to be brought in before the land could be cultivated. In the province of Tehuacan, for instance, corn prospered thanks to irrigation canals. In the Andes, around Cuzco, Pisac, and numerous other Inca sites, irrigation canals were built across ravines and tunneled through mountains.

Tlaloc, god of the long-awaited rain, was certainly the first god to be worshiped by the farmers. In the Colombian Andes, in the Three River area above San Augustin, a 150-square-foot rock was carved as a monument, sculpted in the very bed of a torrent. The whole area was devoted to the cult of the waters that hurtled down the mountain slopes toward the oceans.

In the fourteenth century (about the time of the Hundred Years' War), the first Aztecs developed the area around Lake Texcoco. They dug ditches, raised the ground, made dams with bundles of brushwood, and began to build dikes.

...ources were limited and heat oppressive in the humid Amazon ...est. Game was rare and the area was sparsely populated. These ...ans struggle to make a clearing, using fire. They use stone hoes ...plant a few yams or cassava.

...rn is the primary resource of this village located in the altiplano of ... Andes. The adobe houses with terraced roofs cling to the shel-...ng overhang of the mountain. A large area for drying is being pre-...ed. Villagers spread out and turn the heavy gold corn with ...oden rakes.

Opposite Huayna Picchu, at 7,000 feet above sea level, Inca farmers work on the steep slopes of Machu Picchu. They dig narrow level steps and build low supporting walls to make terraces called anden-nes.

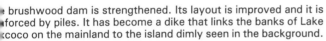

...e brushwood dam is strengthened. Its layout is improved and it is ...forced by piles. It has become a dike that links the banks of Lake ...xcoco on the mainland to the island dimly seen in the background.

People are on the way to Tenochtitlan, the "amphibious" capital of the Aztecs. The small square reed hut is an essential element of cleanliness in a city that has no sewage system.

Working with Stone

There was limited use of metal in the pre-Columbian societies. The materials and the technology they used had flourished in Europe in the Neolithic age 3,000 years before. Europeans began to use bronze about 2000 B.C. and iron about 1000 B.C. The Americas would have to wait until the arrival of Columbus to discover these metals.

Although the techniques of metal working had not yet developed, the pre-Columbians were still able to create architectural masterpieces in stone. To work the stone they had to rely on such primitive techniques as wearing it down. This made the use of metal unnecessary but it also took a great deal of time.

The industrious Olmecs cut hard jade, their favorite stone, with a string, used as a saw, and wet sand. The Incas split huge blocks of stone by hollowing out mortises, then fitting the mortises with tenons of damp wood that eventually expanded and forced the stone to crack. The Toltec builders of Tula used interlocking tenons and mortises, like the builders of the huge megaliths of Stonehenge near Salisbury, in England. Very heavy stones (some of them weighed several tons) were given a perfect fit by having their connecting surfaces ground with a millstone made of sandstone. Rock crystal, the hardest kind of basalt, could be worked with a quartz chisel and a mallet. Polishing added a perfect finish.

Ordinary stones such as silex in Europe and obsidian in the Americas were used to work easier and more common materials, like wood or bone. They were extracted in open pits and quarries where collective work was the rule. Obsidian eventually became commercially valuable. First bartered and later traded, it stood as the enduring symbol of stone craftmanship in the Americas.

Workers representing all the different crafts are gathered here on the Mayan site at Palenque to build the palace. Architects, stone cutters, carpenters, and stucco sculptors work feverishly. The time is 800 A.D. Charlemagne was then ruling in Europe.

28

...sps of smoke are still drifting from the sides of a volcano near Po-...atepetl. First, these men pry out and cut blocks of hard black ob-...an, a glittering, volcanic rock that splits easily. Then they carry ...se rocks on their backs in large nets suspended from headbands.

...e pre-Columbian world had no metal, except for the gold and silver ...t were reserved for princely ornaments. It was still living in the ...tlithic Age. This artisan is hollowing and chipping at a block of ...alt with a wooden mallet and a quartz chisel.

The pale-green jade was a sacred stone for the Olmecs. Their sta-tues, masks, pendants, and jewelry were made from jade. Since it is very hard, the Olmecs sawed it with a string whose constant seesaw motion dug a groove that was kept constantly wet and sandy.

Shortly before 1000 A.D. the Toltecs erected this pillar, representing their god Quetzalcoatl, to support one of their temples. A master arti-san is carving out the tenon that will fit into the mortise of the cylin-der next to it.

...e Olmecs of the tiny island of La Venta used the same neolithic ...hnique to sculpt this monumental head, more than six feet high ...d weighing twenty tons. In the background, men are unloading an ...cut block of basalt from a balsa raft. The block was hewn from a ...rry a hundred miles away.

The Secrets of the Architects

To construct their first temples, builders used a method of piling up huge mounds of earth. This is how the first American pyramid was formed, the circular, four-level pyramid at Cuicuilco. The pyramids and high platforms of the Olmecs of La Venta and Kaminal Juyu, near Guatemala City, were also made of earth, as are the gigantic mounds in North America. The erection of monoliths, stones cut from a single block and weighing several tons each, seems to have been the second great stage of construction in all monumental architecture. It can be found throughout many parts of the world.

The American monoliths were not merely rough hewn rocks. Very often they were shaped, raised up with the help of stakes, and even sculpted, as in the case of the Gate of the Sun on the Andean high plateau. It has been estimated that about a year of work was necessary to create just one of the huge statues on Easter Island.

The third stage in the development of the builders'

craft, one that was both logical and chronological, came when they started forming piles of raw blocks of stone, then of dressed stone and clay bricks. The Inca architects and stone cutters used stones weighing several tons, especially for the bases of their walls. But true architecture went far beyond this stage. Workers began to use the tenon and mortise invented by foresters and woodcutters (the end of one plank fitted into the socket of another). Stones could be cut and fitted together in the same way. The colossal figures on Easter Island can therefore be viewed as enormous building exercises.

The use of supporting frames, also learned from the woodcutters, allowed the construction of vaulted roofs, and the execution of the great monumental borders that decorate Uxmal, Chichen Itza, and Palenque.

In the eleventh or twelfth century, the citizens of Tiahuanaco, the capital of Bolivia, watch as the Gate of the Sun is raised. This monolith made of andesite is nine feet high, twelve feet wide and weighs almost twenty tons.

is slow procession of workers, carrying forty to sixty pounds of rth on their backs in nets suspended from bands around their ads, will build the circular pyramid of Cuicuilco, near Mexico City about 300 B.C. This, the first monument, measured 400 feet in diameter and had four levels, one on top of the other.

In the hills of the Ohio River, a tributary of the Mississippi, the Hopewell Indians built numerous mounds where they buried their dead. Two thousand years ago, they built this immense serpentine mound, half a mile long and ninety feet high.

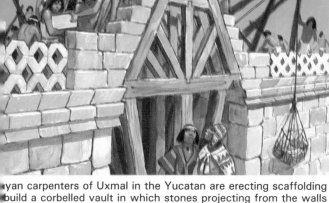

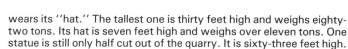

yan carpenters of Uxmal in the Yucatan are erecting scaffolding build a corbelled vault in which stones projecting from the walls port beams across them. Masons are finishing the stone frieze th diamond-shaped patterns which are characteristic of Uxmal.

Cuzco's Inca walls fit together extraordinarily well. Huge, many-sided blocks weighing several tons were put in place with the help of tenons. Two workers are polishing a block with millstones and wet sand.

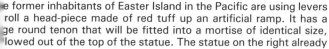

e former inhabitants of Easter Island in the Pacific are using levers roll a head-piece made of red tuff up an artificial ramp. It has a ge round tenon that will be fitted into a mortise of identical size, lowed out of the top of the statue. The statue on the right already

wears its "hat." The tallest one is thirty feet high and weighs eighty-two tons. Its hat is seven feet high and weighs over eleven tons. One statue is still only half cut out of the quarry. It is sixty-three feet high.

Tenochtitlan, the Metropolis of the Americas

The ancient city of Tenochtitlan, the future Mexico City, has been called the "Venice of Mexico." It could more justly have been called the "Venice of the New World," because of its wealth and its geographic location. And in fact the two "Venices" enjoyed political power and intellectual glory at about the same time.

The Aztec capital was uniquely situated on reinforced islands in the lagoon, and was connected to the mainland by three long, elevated causeways. With an estimated population of some 300,000, Tenochtitlan in the fifteenth century was the largest metropolis in the Americas. It was also the most modern and opulent city of its time. Its plan followed an even and perfect grid pattern radiating from the main square. The square itself was dominated by the Great Pyramid, the twin temples of which celebrated Tlaloc, the rain god, and Huitzilopochtli, the solar god of war. The areas near the square were filled with superb residences, with enclosed flower gardens.

On the outskirts, the craft and trade distri[ct] teemed with people. Strollers and merchants, porte[rs] wearing headbands to carry enormous loads in nets [on] their backs, all bustled about in the daily markets. Sim[il]ilar markets filled the flagstoned squares that led to th[e] Great Temple. Small shopkeepers such as barber[s], scribes, and tailors did their business in tiny booth[s]. There were also feather-workers and sculptors wh[o] worked with semi-precious stones, onyx, and obsidia[n]. Blades, almost two feet long, were for sale. Shops we[re] filled to overflowing with gold and silver jewelry, tu[r]quoise ornaments, quetzal feathers, Mitla fabrics, ony[x] pendants from Puebla, and jaguar, puma, or ocel[ot] furs. Less fashionable shops offered more necessar[y] consumer products. All the wealth of the Aztec worl[d] was concentrated in its prestigious capital.

Tenochtitlan's high priest was responsible for the worship of Tlalo[c] at the Great Pyramid. Here he returns from Acatitlan (now Santa Ce[-] cilia), a neighboring village, where he has been dedicating a temple t[o] Tlaloc. He is carried on a palanquin on his way back to the capital.

is scribe transcribes the commercial accounts of his clients on ave leaves. They sit in a tiny booth on a street corner. Aztecs used complex set of writing symbols called glyphs, and counted in pres. A point meant "1," a bar "5."

The small town of Copilco near Lake Texcoco is indeed a Mexican Pompei! Huddled at the base of the volcano Xitli, it suffered from many eruptions. The last one, in about the year 300, buried the town in cinders and lava. But even twenty-five feet of lava could not bury the pyramid of Cuicuilco.

ians did not have much body hair. Nevertheless, a barber has just shed shaving his customer with a razor-sharp obsidian blade. This ber is holding up a mirror, also of polished obsidian, to let his cli- appreciate the results of his work.

ew miles from Tenochtitlan, the Tlatelolco market carried every n one might think of. Five hundred years ago, it was the busiest rket of the Aztec world. Everything was for sale, including slaves quired during the latest feuds with neighboring tribes. Around their

Various products of the Andean area are on display here—gorgeous ocelot furs, brought from the Amazon forest; narrow belts with llama hair trimmings; and bundles of delicate, colorful feathers. In the background is a modest display of ceramic household wares.

necks, these slaves are wearing yokes—heavy wooden rings, locked at the joint by wooden bolts that are firmly tied to the bamboo pillory. The slave trader is touting his merchandise.

Conquering Trade Routes

America, from north to south, has always present[ed] an extraordinary array of terrains. This is why t[he] pre-Columbians had to overcome almost insu[r]mountable obstacles before they could set up tra[de] routes. The continent was huge, the population w[as] sparse, and the resources fairly plentiful in all r[e]gions. As a result, people had no natural inclinati[on] or great need to trade with each other. From the A[t]lantic Ocean to the Rocky Mountains, the Indi[an] tribes confined their trading to some barter of loc[al] products. Furs were exchanged for corn, and e[s]parto grass containers or ceramics for salt.

The high plateaus stood at 6,000 to 9,000 fe[et] above sea level, locked between huge mounta[in] ranges that towered at 16,000 to 18,000 feet. The[se] determined the course of the first settlements on t[he] continent. The immigrants lingered in regio[ns] where the climate was more agreeable than the h[ot] and humid weather they experienced on the shor[es] and in the coastal plains. In spite of the difficulty [of] traveling along these high plateaus, surrounded [as] they were by steep mountains, trade gradually d[e]veloped, spurred by the growth of the great pr[e-] Columbian civilizations. Since the wheel was u[n]known and there were no animals to haul goods, t[he] traders walked, carrying their goods on their back[s.]

Exotic fruits, peppers (always in demand[),] cotton, cocoa, latex balls collected by tapping t[he] trunks of hevea trees, and fish straight out of t[he] warm waters of the gulf of Veracruz, were all ca[r]ried on foot up to the Mexican high plateaus, [to] feed, clothe, and enrich Tenochtitlan. Guano fro[m] the islands of the Pacific was carried across t[he] harsh Andes, along with fish and shells, to fertili[ze] the lands of the Incas and provide Cuzco with [a] more varied diet. Precious silver from the Ande[an] mines was dispatched to the Inca cities in heavi[ly] guarded convoys. Only one animal, the llama, ne[xt] of kin to the camel, was domesticated in Sou[th] America. This resilient animal, which lived in t[he] high Andean mountains, could carry up to nine[ty] pounds on its back and walk sixty miles a day. [It] was the only pack animal. But in America huma[n] carriers were resilient too!

Long caravans of traders like these walked across the deep v[al]leys of the Andes on narrow bridges made of vines, swingi[ng] dangerously above swift-flowing torrents.

...a was a twelve-hour walk from Tenochtitlan. At this very busy ...et the valley's fruits and vegetables were sold along with bas-...ork and piles of ceramics made for domestic use. Many of the ...els were made from rough red clay, and some were glazed in red ...lack.

Blankets are piled up in this shop. Their gorgeous colors and elabo-rate Aztec patterns tantalize this customer from Tenochtitlan. The shop also carries serapes, ponchos made of single blankets with holes in the middle for the head. They are popular garments.

...cooking stone, heated over a fire of glowing embers, is white-...The idea of eating a savory corn tortilla stuffed with hot pepper ...e is tempting.

A long, twisting caravan winds its way through the Andean alti-plano, at 9,000 feet above sea level. These merchants and their heavily loaded llamas may be following one of the many Inca routes, paths used constantly by official messengers carrying orders to every corner of the empire.

...imilco's floating market probably began with the arrival of the ...settlers on the Mexican plateau. Humans here found fertile, eas-...orked land, and the abundant water of a lagoon, in the middle of

a plateau where sprouting cactuses gave warning of droughts. Long, flat-bottomed boats, carrying fruits and vegetables, circulated among the garden-islands, on the canals that crisscrossed the area.

Feather Masks and Alpaca Cloth

Artisans demonstrated ingenuity and great creativity in the many small businesses they ran. Clay, soaked and kneaded, then compressed in wooden frames, was dried in the sun to make the adobes (bricks) used to build houses. The same clay was used to make drinking vessels and cooking utensils.

Other artisans turned plant fibers into cloth. They made fine cotton cloth with fiber from the hot tropical regions of the Gulf of Veracruz. Coarser or stronger cloth was made from tougher vegetable fibers, extracted from different native agaves like maguey or sisal. In the Mitla area, the Mixtecs were famous for their textiles. Weaving bars, too primitive to be called looms, were held by the craftworkers. Supporting ropes were tied to a tree or hooked to a pole to support the warp. The weaver passed the wooden shuttle alternately over and under the warp threads, to make the weft. The fabric thus created was rather narrow since its width was limited to the expanse of the weaver's

arms. Its decorative patterns were simple, consisting of parallel, oblique, and V-shaped stripes of different colors. To get a wider piece of weaving several strips of cloth would be sewn together. If they were accurately aligned they produced a hatched pattern. Sometimes much more complicated patterns, such as diamond shaped or Greek key patterns, emerged because of clumsy or hasty sewing together of the different strips. Such unintentionally created patterns were systematically repeated thereafter. The weaver used either vegetable fibers from the native agave, or different kinds of wool, from the domesticated llama or the wild vicuna. The alpaca, a domesticated variety of guanaco, provided wool for thick, warm woolens.

Only very narrow strips of fabric could be woven on this simple Mi loom. These strips, if they were sewn together carelessly, produc patterns that the weaver did not expect.

long leaves of the maguey would be soaked for several days.
y the most resilient and woody fibers would survive such treat-
nt. Afterwards they were combed and woven. The fabric ob-
ed was very sturdy.

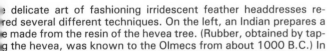

s unusual task is not for everyone! On a tributary of the Maranon,
Amazon Indian attempts to tame an alligator. The idea is to teach
alligators, which are sometimes eighteen feet long, to prefer
gs to human flesh.

e delicate art of fashioning irridescent feather headdresses re-
red several different techniques. On the left, an Indian prepares a
e made from the resin of the hevea tree. (Rubber, obtained by tap-
g the hevea, was known to the Olmecs from about 1000 B.C.) In

The Missouri Indians lived on the vast, grassy Western plains of
North America. Here, one of their hunters paints the story of his feats
on a stretched-out buffalo hide. The Indian woman is scraping another hide to prepare it for other such masterpieces.

the foreground, another worker prepares frames made of reed or
light wood, and classifies the multicolored feathers. On the right, yet
another worker assembles and glues the feathers onto these frames.
He creates headdresses, masks, crowns, and feather mosaics.

Gold and Silver Ornaments

The pre-Columbians loved to adorn themselves as human beings have since the beginning of time. Many hard stones, such as onyx, jade, and even rock crystal, which is extra hard, were sought to make beads shaped like balls, olives, or discuses.

Gold, since it was scarcer than such common materials as wood, clay, or stone, had a symbolic and religious meaning for the Indians of the Andes. Gold symbolized the sun, the god Inti, but was also considered suitable for more practical or everyday purposes. Along with gold, the only other metals the Indians knew were silver and copper. Gold, however, was reserved for the ruling classes, the political leaders and the priests.

Gold was used extensively for the making of jewelry. Pendants and breast plates, or pectorals, were decorated with endlessly repeated geometric patterns. To make the gold masks that symbolically linked the dead to the sun itself, the Indians hammered gold into sheets and then molded the sheets on wooden models representing

humans. The nobles and the priests ate from golden bowls. Sometimes the walls of their houses and their temples were adorned with sheets of gold.

However, this omnipresent gold did not have the social and financial significance that it had come to have in the Old World. The conquistadors did not think of gold as a metal for making dishes or coating the stones of a monument. They saw it as a means to acquire absolute power. When they conquered the New World, they demanded an enormous ransom in exchange for their prisoner, the Great Inca. They caused two 600-cubic-foot rooms to be filled with silver objects and one 300-cubic-foot room with gold ones, all broken, crushed, and compacted, to take as little space as possible. The conquistadors greedily stole every bit of gold they could lay their hands on.

A convoy of heavily loaded llamas is escorted by Inca archers in the Montaro gorges north of Lima, Peru. The caravan carries silver ingots, extracted from the mines high up in the mountains.

the Amazon, in the Tumuc Humac mountains, Indians use a
, a flat wicker basin, to pick up gold deposits from the stream.
aking the basin in the water, they eliminate the grains of sand.
esidue is gold dust which is heavier than sand.

A very fine dust eats at the lungs of these miners in a narrow, airless
gallery of a silver mine in the Andes, at the incredible altitude of
15,000 feet. One of them loosens a few chunks of silver ore with a
pick while his helper sorts them out.

priest who was buried in the necropolis of Monte Alban wore a
pectoral representing the God of Death. On the left hand side,
hown eleven small embossed cupules (cups) and the diagram of
use. These give the day and ''month'' of the year: 11, House.

Gold was worked with a hammer. Pure gold was hammered for hours
until it became a thin sheet which was then plated and beaten onto a
wooden model of a human face. Inca and Aztec masks very often
looked like their models.

is the color of young, green corn and had religious value which
transferred to figurines made with it. On the right, an artisan
a mallet and chisel cuts a block of jade into pieces. His compan-
ores holes in the pieces with the aid of a bow. To do so, first he

moves the bow back and forth, then gives it a circular motion to turn
the drill and pierce the jade. The young girl enjoys trying on the necklaces that have already been made.

From Birth to Marriage

In all pre-Columbian civilizations, from the Indians in Brazil or Tierra del Feugo who gathered roots and berries, to the hunting Mandan Indians and the Eskimos, life's important events were organized, celebrated, and recorded. The Mandans had rites of initiation to celebrate a boy's passage from adolescence into manhood, and his coming of age as a warrior. Fasts, dances, and bloody rites had to be performed. The youth had to show that he was immune to fatigue and pain and worthy at last of being a man. When an old Eskimo woman realized that she was becoming a burden to her clan, she would retire of her own accord to the tundra to die.

Be they Aztec, Maya, or Inca, the urban civilizations, those in direct contact with the Spaniards, are best known to us now. They possessed priceless manuscripts, stories transcribed from their native languages with a wealth of naive and accurate imagery. They are quite literally Aztec cartoons that enable us to trace Aztec daily life from birth to death.

Fathers were entrusted with the education of their sons; mothers, with that of their daughters. Little girls learned how to use the spindle to spin wool, from the time they were six years old. Between the ages of six and nine, the children of high-ranking officials entered the *calmecac*, an institution that was half-school, half-seminary. These schools prepared them either for priesthood or for high positions of state. But many children attended only the local school, the *telpochcalli*, where religious education, fasts, and penance played a less prominent part than at the calmecac, while military songs and exercises were emphasized. All Aztec children went to school. Even children from poor families, if they had merit, could attend the calmecac and thus aspire to prestigious positions in the social hierarchy.

The all-important wedding day finally comes. When the bride and groom come together, they immediately tie the ends of each other's girdles together as a symbol of their union. The guests bring presents and good wishes.

nidwife presents a newborn baby to the family and the servants.
t, she prays for him, then washes him in the purifying water of
goddess Chachiuhtlicue, mother and sister of the gods. The child
be consecrated within the next four days.

With their cloaks smartly knotted on their right shoulders, these two
young boys go to school accompanied by a household slave. They
are entering the calmecac. The priests will teach them how to speak
well, to salute, to bow, and to have self-control.

om early infancy young girls were destined to serve in the temple.
me of them got a very strict education for a few years. Then,
hen they were about twenty, they could ask their masters and the
mily council for permission to get married. Other girls stayed in the

temple and would be given the much envied title of priestess. They
became expert at creating magnificent embroideries, took part in the
rites, offered incense to the gods, and learned the sacred chants that
accompanied the great religious ceremonies.

rious corporal punishments were meted out at school as well as at
me. Here an angry father punishes his son who has failed at the
lmecac. He holds the child above a fire of burning green pimentos
hich produce unbearably stinging smoke.

Practical exercises, that were sometimes very rough, played an important part in the young Aztecs' military training. They were taught
how to fight. Here two youngsters fight bitterly with arms and
shields adapted to their size, while their coach watches them.

Games and Celebrations

The game of *tlachtli*, or pelota, probably began with the Olmecs, in hevea country. The game was played on a large field, shaped like an elongated H. Two teams vied with each other to make a heavy rubber ball pass through two vertical stone rings fixed into a wall nine feet above the ground. It looked a little like a basketball game, played with vertical baskets. Players could touch the ball only with their hips, elbows, or knees. Later the tlachtli took on a religious significance. The ball's path was identified with the sun's orbit in the sky, and the passing of the ball through the ring became the symbol of the sun reaching its zenith.

Large numbers of people enjoyed the tlachtli game. Cities like Chichen Itza, Tajin, Uxmal, Tikal, and Copan had several arenas, the size of which depended on the amount of religious significance attributed to the game. Betting was heavy, and the stakes ranged from feathers and clothing to slaves. For the players the stake was enormous: death to the losers!

The game of *volador*, played in the Gulf of Veracruz, was peaceful but it too involved worship of the sun. The beginning of the game was static. Players danced, sang and played music on a platform at the top of a ninety foot pole. Then came the "flight." With their bodies covered with feathers to make them look like birds, four dancers jumped from the platform, held by long ropes they had carefully coiled and folded like the strings of a parachute. They quite literally hovered, head downward, going around and around in ever widening, ever slower, circles until, in a magnificent recovery, they finally reached the ground.

In the Yucatan peninsula, an enthusiastic crowd jams the Chichen Itza arena, 200 feet long, the largest in all the Americas. Two teams vie with each other to make the hard rubber ball go through the vertical ring.

recent discovery of frescoes in the temple of Bonampak makes it
[pos]sible for us to imagine and reconstruct the lavish Mayan ceremo-
[ni]es. Heralds blow through wooden trumpets. Their slow, insistent
[chan]t announces the imminent arrival of the procession of priests.

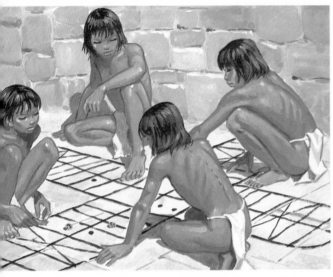

[Th]ese little Indians are playing at *patolli*, a game played with beans.
[Lin]es on the ground in the form of a cross define fifty-two spaces
[tha]t stand for the years in the Aztec century.

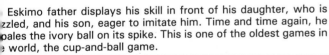

[An] Eskimo father displays his skill in front of his daughter, who is
[pu]zzled, and his son, eager to imitate him. Time and time again, he
[im]pales the ivory ball on its spike. This is one of the oldest games in
[th]e world, the cup-and-ball game.

The *volador* dance is a typical ceremony of the Gulf of Veracruz. At
the top of a long pole, the leader of the dance plays the *chirimaya* (a
bamboo flute) and the *tun* (a drum). Underneath him four bird-
dancers, swing from the pole by ropes attached at the waist.

The cadence of the *balafon*, at first slow and muffled, then hurried
and loud, gives rhythm to the dance of these lance-bearing warriors
of Patagonia. Narrow planks, fixed to the tops of calabashes of various sizes, resound when hit by two clubs made of hard wood.

Medicine for the Body and Mind

One of the conquistadors, Bernardino de Sahagun, acknowledged and praised the Aztecs' medical knowledge: "They were highly experienced and had great knowledge of the properties and virtues of herbs . . . They invented medicine." At the markets, an incredible array of plants, seeds, roots, barks, and mushrooms was available. The Aztecs, as well as the Incas, knew how to set fractured bones and immobilize the wounded limb with splints, held by vines or plant fibers.

They also knew how to extract a broken arrowhead from a wound, either by suction or by making an incision with a sharp obsidian blade. The wound was then skillfully stitched with sharp thorns and maguey fibers, used as needle and thread.

Mental illnesses were feared because of their mysterious origins. The Peruvians practiced clever trepanning to remove brain tumors. They thought that opening up the patient's skull would allow the evil spirits locked inside the brain to escape. They scraped the bones of the skull with an obsidian knife to isolate the diseased area, pierced the bone with a stone awl, and removed a round or square piece of the skullcap. In the Cuzco area, archeologists have discovered a skull bearing the scars of four trepannings, all four of them successfully healed. The patient had survived.

The gods and the spirits were often called upon to support medicine. The weirdest and most mysterious rites played a role, sometimes with very beneficial effect, on the mental health of the patient. In Tierra del Fuego, the high priest often chanted to summon the ancestral spirit of his patient to cure him. The Medicine Man of the Crow Indians advised his clients to take a steam bath as an "offering to the Sun."

Steam baths purified the body by allowing it to sweat out all of its evil spirits. Outside this bathhouse a huge furnace heats its walls and brings water to the boil. Servants brought the boiling water inside in large pots and splashed it against the already heated walls of the room where the bathers were enclosed.

is patient fell from a mango tree while picking fruit and broke his
. The "doctor" immobilizes his leg with splints, made of balsa
od, and ties them carefully with vines. As a result, the broken
e will mend rapidly.

Bleeding a patient was as common a practice among Mexican Indians as it would become in Europe two centuries later. They lanced
the skin with an obsidian blade and kept the incision open with
thorns from the maguey cactus to allow the blood to flow easily.

e wound on this man's left arm is dangerously infected. He tore
 flesh open when he fell on sharp and dirty rocks. The healing pro-
ss will be speeded up by dressing the wound with the sap of a vir-
al miracle tree, the Yin tree, that helps to soothe pain.

This old man is in the throes of a frightening epileptic fit which the
Indians believed to be caused by evil spirits taking possession of the
body. Jerking uncontrollably, he is restrained by an aide who holds
him firmly while his "doctor" makes him swallow a soothing potion.

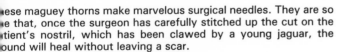

ese maguey thorns make marvelous surgical needles. They are so
e that, once the surgeon has carefully stitched up the cut on the
tient's nostril, which has been clawed by a young jaguar, the
ound will heal without leaving a scar.

No one knows why the sick man has lost consciousness, so drastic
measures must be taken. A turkey, one of the few domesticated animals on the continent, will be sacrificed and the patient will be made
to swallow the juice of its salivary glands.

Life to the Rhythm of the Stars

In about the year 1000 A.D. a curious stairway, built in the form of a helix, could be observed at Chichen Itza. It led to an observation chamber at the top of a huge tower. The observatory was rectangular and was equipped with seven very narrow slits overlooking the countryside. They were used as sightings to make precise observations: the direction of the south; the position of the moon at its setting; the directions of the sun at sunset on March 21 and on September 22, when days are as long as nights (these days are called equinoxes); and on the summer and winter solstices, when days are at their longest or shortest.

The Americas did not lag behind the Old World in the realm of thought. The Indians were remarkable mathematicians. The Mayas had a base 20 system of calculus, using three signs only, including zero. As a matter of fact the zero, known in Sri Lanka by about 1000 B.C., was unknown in Europe until the Arabs introduced it when they invaded in the eighth century.

Through a real genius for the manipulation of figures, the Mayas achieved much greater accuracy in astronomical calculations than people did in the West. They knew how to use whole numbers up to more than a billion!

The Aztecs knew the discus, as is proved by the large solar calendar of Tenochtitlan, but not its application to everyday life, that is, its use as a wheel. Strangely enough though, on the Mexican plateau some toys have been found with fragile clay wheels. The Aztecs also adopted the Mayan religious calendar that divided time into cycles of fifty-two years, the Aztec century. They found in this calendar some guide marks that helped them understand and predict the occurrence of natural phenomena. The Mayan calendar was more precise than ours.

Let us climb the stairway leading to the great observatory of Chichen Itza with these Mayan priests. Later, the Spaniards would rename the monument the *caracol* because of its interior spiral stairway shaped like a snail's shell.

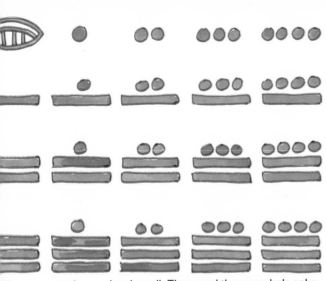

The Mayas counted marvelously well. They used three symbols only: [po]int for one, a line for the number five, and an elongated, shell-[shap]ed sign for no value or zero. This table gives the signs for zero to [nine]teen.

[Lla]mas file along on this Andean path. This merchant is counting the [floc]ks on a *kipu*, a three-foot long rope with knotted cords of various [length]s and colors hanging from it. One simple knot stands for the unit, [and] the more complicated ones go up to nine.

[This] Aztec warrior is contemplating a huge calendar stone. Some of [its] symbols stand for days of the year, while others contain informa-[tion] predicting solar eclipses. Toniatiuh, the blood-thirsty sun god, is [in th]e center.

A priest offers incense and pays homage at this Mayan stela. The glyphs on the sides are still undeciphered. The tallest known stela is thirty feet high, and was built about 771 A.D. in Quinga, in southern Guatemala.

On the sacred square of Machu Picchu, 800 feet above sea level in the central Andes, rises the "Solar Stone." This strangely shaped monolith cut from rock, was the very heart of the city. Every day, Inca priests came here to celebrate the rising of the sun.

Deities

The religious beliefs of the Aztecs evolved slow[ly] throughout the ages as they added the gods of pe[o]ples they had conquered to their own pantheo[n]. This is why the Aztecs were perceived as the mo[st] religious of all the Indian groups. In their distant o[r]igins, a couple of gods, supreme above all other[s], embodied fire and earth. The old fire god was re[p]resented as an old man somberly guarding a br[a]zier. At mealtimes, he was usually offered a fe[w] tortilla crumbs and some drops of pulque. The o[ld] goddess Coatlicue wore an ample skirt, made [of] threatening snakes, symbols of the depths of t[he] underworlds. Because growing corn and oth[er] crops required much rain on the arid high platea[u] of Mexico, the cult of Tlaloc arose, the ancient g[od] of rain and water. He was one of the major gods [of] Teotihuacan, the city of the gods. In the very o[ld] pyramid dedicated to the cult of Quetzalcoatl, Tl[a]loc alternated with the plumed serpent. His bi[g] round eyes, so typical of the god, were made of o[b]sidian circles. But the most famous of the gods wa[s] undoubtedly the divine plumed serpent, Quetza[l]coatl, at once a symbol of death (he was a snak[e]) and of rebirth (he wore the shimmering feathers [of] the quetzal bird).

The Aztecs revered the stars. They thought [of] themselves as the sun's people and worshiped th[e] solar disc. They offered him "precious water," that is to say human blood, so that the world mig[ht] continue to survive. Each person's destiny wa[s] closely linked to the stars presiding over his or h[er] birth. Reconciling the worship due to the gods wi[th] the demands of their own astrological signs was th[e] overriding concern of all Aztecs, and absorbed th[e] better part of their resources and energy.

The temple dedicated to the dead sun and to Tlaloc, the ra[in] god, stands on top of the pyramid of Acatitlan. The high priest [is] calling upon the gods, begging them to continue the lif[e] sustaining cycle of the sun and of the blessed rain that enabl[es] the corn to grow.

old fire god, most ancient of the gods, is shown as a wrinkled old ٦, wearing a brazier on his head. He was probably copied after the ;anoes, the cones of which are natural pyramids, towering above lagoon of Tenochtitlan. A priest watches over the flame in this ١bolic hearth.

; solemn procession of priests marches through a subterranean ٤am in a deep grotto. They carry an urn holding the ashes of a :h admired chief which will be placed by dozens of similar ones.

In the ninth century, when Pacal, the ruler-priest of Palenque, died he was buried, as Egyptians were, in a sarcophagus cut from one stone, which lay in the crypt underneath the Pyramid of the Inscriptions. A hugh slab of stone is being rolled over the tomb to seal it.

At the end of the thirteenth century, the Incas roamed the Andean plateaus, in search of a place where they could settle down. Their chief, Manco Capac, bearer of a golden staff, strikes it into the ground. On this spot he is founding the city of Cuzco.

Descendants of the Sun

The important part human sacrifices played in the Aztec culture repelled the Europeans. Since the Aztecs were the sons and daughters of the sun, they had to feed him with their own blood. The victims were many and these human sacrifices were the target of vast amounts of political and religious propaganda. The Spanish bishops used them as an excuse to justify their ruthless conquest of this civilization by calling it a crusade. But were the Aztec human sacrifices higher in number than the victims of the Inquisition or than the casualties of the religious wars that bloodied Europe in that same sixteenth century? Did they exceed the numbers of gladiators sent to the circus games by Imperial Rome?

Archeologists have found the remains of thirteen men, eight women, and twenty-one children, thrown into the depths of the *cenote* (sinkhole) at Chichen Itza in the heart of Mayan country, as offerings to the rain god. As for the Aztecs, such terrible practices encouraged their fratricidal wars since they felt justified in taking more prisoners, intended for sacrifice. When

peace intervened, they invented the War of Flowers. This was literally a tournament held to find victims for their demanding gods. Yet, startling as it may seem, many Aztecs were willing victims. Every year, a young man, who had to be the epitome of perfection, gave his life to Tezcatlipoca, the symbol of the constellation of the Great Bear of the night sky. He was chosen from among many aspiring candidates to symbolize the god himself. So he died as a god, facing his own image, in his own temple, to save the world. In an act of ritual cannibalism, the priest or the faithful ate the very flesh of the god in bloody communion. All, whether they were prisoners, slaves, or volunteers, sacrificed their lives to make sure that their afterlife would be happy.

Rather than be condemned to a life of hard toil, this captive prefers to die on the sacrificial altar, thus assuring his eternal happiness. He is stretched out on the stone, still covered with the blood of other sacrifices. The high priest slashes his chest open with the long obsidian blade of his knife and rips out his heart to offer it to the sun.

Mandan woman from Missouri is still young. A Sioux warrior
killed her husband with his tomahawk. As a sign of bereave-
[m]ent, she is going to let the tribal sorcerer cut off one of her fingers
[with] a stroke of his stone axe.

[Rou]gh physical tests were part of an adolescent's rites of passage.
[The]se young Mandans are enduring a hanging test. The ropes that
[hold] them are tied to wooden pegs inserted in their flesh.

The cenote of Chichen Itza in Yucatan was a huge natural well, 180
feet wide, that opened in the limestone. Chac, the Mayan rain god,
was worshiped here. This young girl, bedecked in all her finery, is
hurled into the pit as a sacrifice to ensure the coming of the rain.

[The] highest pyramid of Tenochtitlan, the Aztec capital, has three
[stair]ways of 120 steps each. On the right, the temple of Huitzilo-
[poch]tli, god of the sun at noon, faces the temple of Tlaloc, the god of
rain, on the left. Mass sacrifices, there were 20,000 victims in four
days, are taking place on the steps.

The War of Flowers

War was a constant reality to the Aztecs. A bellicose spirit animated their daily lives. In fact, war was the only profession that guaranteed spectacular success to those capable of winning every fight. So, the Aztecs were never too young to train for it.

The umbilical cord of a newborn baby was buried under the threshold of the house. If the baby was a boy, the midwife delivered a long speech promising him that he would be a warrior: "You must give the sun enemy blood to drink." At about age six or seven, the child entered the *telpochcalli*, a school that emphasized military training where children were drilled constantly in mock fights. When he was ten, the boy's hair was cut, as a sign of his masculinity and adulthood, except for a short lock at the nape of his neck that was to be cut once he had captured his first prisoner. When he had captured or killed four prisoners, he became a full-fledged citizen, a *tequina*. He then enjoyed the full privileges of citizenship, had to pay his share of taxes, and could

participate in the government and administration of the city. Those who could not make a name for themselves remained common people.

The ultimate dream of a tequina was to enter the highest ranks of the warriors. He dreamed of becoming a jaguar knight or an eagle knight, the most sought-after distinction, since the eagle was the very symbol of the sun, for whom the soldiers were fighting. War was sacred. It was the judgment of the gods. So, the warrior had to provide prisoners destined to be human sacrifices. The so-called War of Flowers was like a tournament with a fixed set of rules. Once the first clash of battle was over, each soldier tried to capture his opponent alive rather than kill him. Aides accompanied the fighters to tie up the conquered enemy who had to be alive in order to face the supreme sacrifice!

This is an uneven battle. These fearless Mayan warriors have taken some helpless, terrified peasants by surprise, in a clearing of the Yucatan peninsula. Since the Mayas have long obsidian-headed spears and their opponents are unarmed, the task is easy.

The war is over but there are not enough prisoners to provide victims for the sacrifices. Tournaments were organized and the losers would be sacrificed. Here the Aztec ''eagle'' attacks a Mixtec warrior with his dangerous spiked spear.

e time of the sacrifice has come. These chiefs gather in front of se doomed to die. The prisoners are thrown on the steps of the nple. The high priest, in a symbolic cloak made of jaguar skins, nounces the death sentence while the dignitaries look on.

ur warriors carry a heavy litter where the Great Inca sits en-oned. He is the almighty ruler of the immense empire that tches along the Andes from north to south. He wears a crimson ge across his forehead as a symbol of his authority. Many and

''Victory'' shouts the Iroquois as he tears the scalp with its hair from the head of his defeated enemy. For the Indians, hair was a symbol of strength, so by scalping an enemy, the victor made the man's strength his own.

fearsome are his warriors, armed with threatening clubs, slings, and bows, as they advance row after dense row upon the enemy. Five thousand such warriors are ready to fight behind the heavy stone ramparts of the citadel that defends Cuzco, the Inca capital.

Gold—Opium of the Conquistadors

"Tierra! Tierra! Land at last!" shouted the poor Spanish sailor on board the *Pinta*. It was October 12, 1492, and the rough crossing had taken sixty five days. Christopher Columbus had reached one of the islands of the Bahamas that he would name San Salvador. When the sun rose, he put on his grand admiral's uniform, disembarked on the island with his companions, kissed the ground and weeping for joy, gave thanks to the Lord. Then, in the name of the Spanish monarchs, he took posses sion of the island.

The 3,000 mile wide ocean, that natural obsta cle separating the New World from the Old, had been spanned. The era of the conquistadors had be gun.

Europeans, hungry for gold and silver, were seeking new and unknown lands. Intense religious zeal drove them to convert people who did not share their beliefs. A combination of these power ful motives was to animate the conquerors who came from Europe. Many "watchdogs of the New World" were to follow in Columbus's footsteps. In 1519, Cortes landed in the Yucatan peninsula and ruled over Aztec Mexico by 1521. Francisco Pi zarro arrived in Peru in 1524. Confident that he would succeed, he confronted the Incas and failed. He failed again in 1526 but succeeded with his third attempt in 1531 and 1532. Atahuallpa, the Great Inca, was finally captured. A ransom was extracted from him and in the end he was strangled. His death rang the death-knell of the Inca empire.

Jacques Cartier, the celebrated Breton from St. Malo, landed near the mouth of the St. Law rence in 1534, and went upriver, to be greeted by Indians still using spears and stone-tipped arrows, much as they would have in the Neolithic Age, 4,000 years before. But the Indians were soon to learn all about gunpowder, bullets, muskets, and guns. Europe had conquered the Americas.

Columbus lands in America. A wooden cross is implanted on the shore before curious native Americans who have arrived in ca noes.

Diego de Landa, the Spanish bishop, has pledged to wipe out the heresy of the New World. He is having all the codices burned in the public squares. These precious manuscripts, inscribed in Indian languages, related the history of the Aztecs and the Mayas.

The last Inca monarch, Atahuallpa, was Pizarro's prisoner. He attempted to buy his freedom. The Incas filled a room in his palace with golden jewelry and offered it to his conquerors, but to no avail. He was condemned to die.

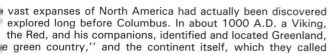

Spaniards occupied Tenochtitlan, and Montezuma, the last em-
or, was their prisoner. The city seethed with resentment and re-
ion. Cortes ordered that Montezuma appear and demand peace.
olley of stones was hurled back at him and eventually killed him.

vast expanses of North America had actually been discovered
explored long before Columbus. In about 1000 A.D. a Viking,
the Red, and his companions, identified and located Greenland,
e green country,'' and the continent itself, which they called

''Vinland,'' or ''land of wine.'' But they found neither spices nor gold
or silver in these territories, only expanses of land to clear and forests
to work. So they left. Five centuries later, the conquistadors looked
more to the south.

THE TEMPLES—A LIVING MEMORY

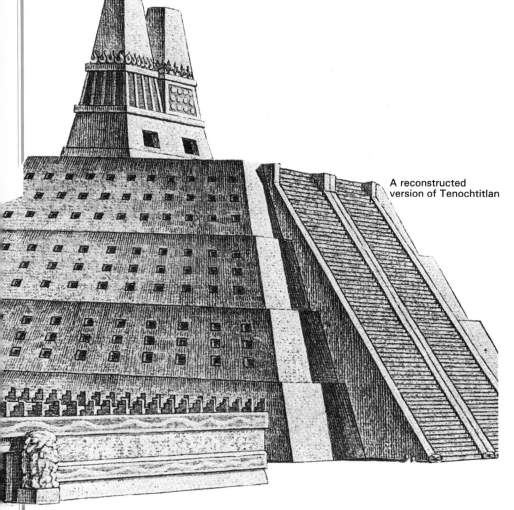

A reconstructed version of Tenochtitlan

Buried civilizations

Cities that had disappeared before the Spanish conquest had better luck than the civilizations to which it laid waste. It is true that they were older. But strangely enough more traces of their past glory have survived. This is true of Teotihuacan, the City of the Gods, near Mexico City, mysteriously abandoned at the beginning of our era. Did the population leave because of soil erosion and the drying up of the San Juan river that flowed through it? If so, the winds would have accumulated enough soil to bury the platforms and temples. In any event, the Toltec invaders who settled in the region not long after, saw only shapeless stumps, leveled off and more or less aligned. They took these mounds for ancient graves, and called the large avenue crossing the city "The Way of the Tombs."

Even the great city of Monte Alban near Oaxaca, before it was carefully excavated, was only a shapeless, leveled hill formed by platforms and bristling with engraved stelae.

The tops of Tikal's high pyramids break through the green curtain of vegetation.

Civilizations laid to waste

Few features of the original aspects of New World culture remain today. At the beginning of the sixteenth century, it was thrust, within a few generations, into the more technical world of European civilization. This brutal transformation wiped out its past. The conquistadors were ruthless in the name of God and Gold. Among other things, they systematically wiped out the city of Tenochtitlan, the Mexican Venice on the banks of Lake Texcoco. They used stones from the Aztec pyramids and temples over again, to build the palaces of their viceroys and the cathedrals of their prelates. As Paul Valery once said: "Civilizations are mortal now."

There are other examples of such recycling in history. Churches in the Middle Ages, for instance, installed marble columns in their crypts, taken from Greek temples or opulent Roman villas. In a later age, quarries of building stone were opened right inside the abbeys of Longport and Royaumont in France. In Peru the conquistadors were content to build their palaces and churches on foundations laid down by the Incas. In fact, when one of the frequent Andean earthquakes occurred, the more recent walls of the palaces collapsed but the Inca foundations endured. In no time at all, new buildings rose once again on these ancient and sturdy foundations. That is why we can still admire the monumental structures of Cuzco today. Because of their massive size, and the way they have been constructed, they are so solid that not even an earthquake can shake them.

56

Tajin, six pyramids in one!

In the great tropical forests, an exuberant vegetation has smothered and swallowed up everything. It has been a double-edged sword, both destroying and preserving. Thus, powerful roots have torn buildings apart, lifting stone slabs from the stairways, and splitting walls open. But sometimes the roots hold the temples together, imprisoning them in a tight, living net. In Guatemala, the 120-foot tall trees of the forest of Peten have completely engulfed the Mayan cities. Only the tops of the highest pyramids of Tikal break through the powerful green blanket of the forest that covers everything. The 140-foot Temple I and the 200-foot Temple IV look, quite literally, like stone islands, lost in a sea of vegetation.

The Pyramid of Niches

When the conquistadors arrived, the large Totonac city of Tajin, in the Gulf of Veracruz, had long been abandoned, literally obliterated by the virgin rain forest. When the site was discovered in 1875, many burial mounds were barely recognizable as such, scattered and lost as they were, in the midst of a thick, impenetrable sea of greenery. These mounds had to be cleared before real excavation work could begin. Digging only began in about 1934 and uncovered pyramids and platforms topped by temples. The most remarkable edifice discovered on this site was certainly the "Pyramid of Niches." Sixty feet high, on a foundation 110 feet square, the pyramid

is oriented according to the cardinal points of the compass. Its six levels are indented by stone-framed niches. As the levels rise each has three niches less than the one immediately below it. All the visible niches (some of them are hidden behind a monumental stairway) add up to a sum total of 365, the number of days in a solar year.

Visitors to Tajin today can see that considerable progress has been made at the archeological digs, which are directed by the National Museum of Mexico. However, there are still several hundred platforms or bases of pyramids hidden under these burial mounds. It is estimated that the archeological sector stretches over millions of square feet, much of it still not cleared or restored. A tunnel dug by archeologists in the west face of the pyramid has revealed its internal structure. We are dealing not with one pyramid but with six, built one on top of the other.

Five more layers of pyramids have been counted, around and above the core of the central pyramid. They are rather like the celebrated *matrushka*, Russian dolls which open up to reveal increasingly smaller dolls. At Uxmal, the structure is different. The two pyramids, built one after the other, are joined together, and the temples are still standing.

The secrets of Cholula

In the Puebla region, the huge pyramid of Cholula has revealed its secrets. A hill, 200 feet high is topped by a church, Santuario de los Remedios, rising above the town. In fact, the hill used to be a pyramid. Nature, erosion, and negligence turned it into a hill. Today, this giant pyramid is 1,500 feet wide and about 200 feet high.

It may at one time have been the largest monument in the world since it had served as a quarry for centuries while the Spanish town of Cholula was being built. Recent archeological digs (five miles of tunnels through the interior) uncovered the older pyramids underneath. The starting points, the roots, so to speak, of all these pyramids, neatly fitted one on top of the other, allow us to understand how they were constructed.

The "fitted" foundations of Cholula

L.-R. NOUGIER

A CURIOUS INVERSION OF CIVILIZATIONS

Opposite:
Chac Mol
(Mayan sculpture)

Below:
Chichen Itza

The Mayas were the first temple builders in the Americas. They built only with stone and without the help of any framework. Usually the temples had three to five small rooms, parallel to each other, and were in fact more like narrow passageways than rooms. They were vaulted by an ingenious arrangement of tiers of stones projecting one above the other. The builders had discovered the technique of corbelling. Large slabs of stone linked the walls of the room and topped off the vault. This is what is called the Maya vault. It is solid, compact and strong, but does not allow for a wide span.

Some very old houses in Southern France, from Quercy to Provence, were built with an identical technique in about 3000 B.C. The temples of the "early Maya" phase were probably built around 800 B.C. They are often remarkably well preserved, as in the case of the Red Temple in Chichen Itza. The rooms are still vaulted and many still have the *cresteria*, a crowning perforated gallery on the roof which gives lightness and elegance to the whole temple.

In the tenth century, the Mayas en-

tered a new phase of monumental building brought about by the influence of the rich and powerful Toltec invaders. (In archeological terms this is called "recent Maya.") Their temples, and their public and religious buildings changed and grew considerably larger. Toltec-Maya architecture was grandiose. Massive walls with

Chichen Itza's Red Temple

few openings, and narrow corbelled vaults, disappeared. Instead, the Maya architects built large, well-lit rooms with wooden floors that opened onto terraces. They were supported on short stone lintels that were soon to be replaced by long wooden beams. At the same time, the vault, spanning narrow corridors, gave way to horizontal wooden frames, covering large areas. The Temple of the Warriors and the area of the Thousand Columns in Chichen Itza are typical examples of the new architectural technique. But the humid climate rotted these great buildings; the wooden roofs and floors collapsed. Only the nine-foot high support columns remain, made of stone drums piled one on top of the other. These relatively recent monuments look like ruins while, on the other side of the road, separating the recent Toltec-Maya zone from the early Maya zone, the ancient temples are almost intact. The old has aged more gracefully and lasted longer than the new. This demonstrates in curious fashion, the strange inversion of the two Mayan civilizations. The ancient one survives, while the newer is only a ruin.

THE MYSTERIES OF THE TOLTEC "CONSTRUCTION GAMES"

The temple of Tlahuizcalpantecuhtli, the Morning Star, towered over the Toltec capital of Tula. The five layers of the pyramid supported a high platform which functioned as a foundation for the temple. This consisted of four tall columns of the type called Atlantes, in the form of Quetzalcoatl, the Morning Star. The columns were named "atlantes" by archeologists because they resembled European atlantes, the plural of Atlas who supported the world. Atlantes are stone figures of men, supporting roofs or parapets. The whole structure was erected about 1000 A.D. and destroyed two or three centuries later by Chichimec invaders. The Atlantes were then taken down from the platform.

Each Atlante is made of four elements joined together by the interplay of mortise and tenon. Recent restoration work led to the recovery of these elements and they were reassembled by the same method. So the Atlantes are reassembled and tower once again over the vast plain of Tula.

The special technique of fitting a tenon into a mortise prepared to receive it raises very exciting archeological problems. Did the Toltecs invent this method or was it previously known? If so, how did it reach the New World and about what time? The awe-inspiring triliths of the great circle of Stonehenge in England are proof that such techniques were used in ancient times. There, two vertical supporting stones with tenons protruding at the tops, are linked by a horizontal lintel whose mortises are hollowed out at each end to fit snugly into the corresponding tenons. This jointing of stone is probably adapted from earlier methods applied to wood, according to an old European forester tradition, and may go back as far as 2000 B.C. Technically, Stonehenge is a remarkable accomplishment. Each element of the jointing weighs fifty tons and the lintel was put in place twenty-five feet above ground, the equivalent of a three-story house. So, one cannot help wondering about a possible relationship between Stonehenge and Tula even though historically the two sites are 3,000 years apart. Actually the problem is infinitely more complex. For the last three to four thousand years, the Western world has known how to saw mortises in the fault lines of rock and insert wooden tenons that, when dampened, force the rock to break. This technique can be found in the building of

megaliths in Brittany, Spain, and all the way down to Egypt. But it can also be found in the Americas, for example, at Machu Picchu.

Another practice consisted of working tenons on stone, to secure ropes tied around it and make it easier to transport. These tenons can be found on Breton megaliths, but they are just as common on the gigantic walls of Cuzco.

Furthermore, on tiny, isolated Easter Island in the Pacific, humans have raised huge statues weighing up to eighty tons. Their heads are crowned by a kind of turban called a *pukao* made of red volcanic tuff. This "hat" is nine feet wide, seven feet high and can weigh up to thirty tons. At one end there is a large tenon that fits into the mortise carved in the top of the statue's head. All this might suggest a technical relationship between Stonehenge, Easter Island, and Tula. But common sense finds more logic in the argument that people, faced with an easy technical problem, habitually tapped the reservoir of their ancestors' experience and came up with the simplest solution, wherever it was needed.

The walls of Sacsahuaman

A STRANGE VOYAGE BETWEEN PAST AND PRESENT

The existence of the pre-Columbian cities raises many archeological problems. But few traditions and relics have survived in the South American countryside. There it is almost as if we are jumping back a thousand years and more, into the past.

For example, for thousands of years in the area surrounding the 10,000-foot-high city of Cuzco, the Chinchero peasants have worked the fertile soil of the altiplano with a wooden swing plow, the fire-hardened head of which digs shallow furrows without turning over the earth. Today, a rudimentary iron plowshare protects the wooden head—not much of a change and very little improvement.

THE MAYAN HOUSE

The Mayan house still exists today—in the forests of Peten and the Yucatan brush. Because it is perfectly adapted to the hot and humid tropical climate of the region, it has remained unchanged over the centuries. (It can be seen sculpted, and framed by a long serpent, on some high reliefs of a temple at Uxmal.) The house is very simple. Rectangular in shape, it is rounded at one end, in much the same way as the apse of a church. Its walls are made of branches stuck into the ground, with a door as the only opening. A dome-shaped roof made of thatched straw covers the house. But this basic shape can have variations. In the Quiriga area, in Honduras, for instance, the walls are made with plaited palm leaves.

Nature itself is stifling here. Yet the Mayan house seems to breathe deeply because the breeze flows freely through it. Furthermore, being built on a platform or on well-drained ground, it is a healthy

building in which to live. The furniture is sparse: a few mats on the floor; a couple of chests to store linen and clothing; a few hooks to hang up the hammocks. This region can indeed be called "the civilization of the hammock." People move around with hammocks in their pockets, sure of always finding two hooks at night, to hang them up.

Changes in the Mayan house are modest. In the Yucatan Peninsula, many houses have an electric bulb dangling from the ceiling. And, once in a while, through a door with its mat tied back, passersby might hear the soft hum of a sewing machine.

THE LAKE PEOPLE

Lake Titicaca in the heart of Andean Peru, 12,000 feet above sea level, was still home, just several decades ago, to the Urus, one of the most naive and most distinctive tribes in the world. As gatherers of roots, and as fishermen, these "lake people" were experts in the many uses of the type of reed that grew there, the totora. The Urus made everything with the totora, the floating platforms they lived on, their huts, and their boats of tightly bundled reeds upturned at the ends. The young children also enjoyed sucking the young shoots of totora, peeled and cut into strips. However, the surviving Urus were all over eighty years old in 1950. Today, travel agencies hire some of the local people to play their part and float once more over the lake on the fragile totora boats.

MALINALCO

In the earliest phases, temples were generally lightly built, just like ordinary dwellings. However, the platforms upon which the temples were erected were made of sturdy terraces, piled one upon the other. Thus, Malinalco is unusual on two counts. First, the great temple and its banistered staircase were carved out of rock. Only the roof resisted this treatment. Second, a traditional Mayan thatched roof tops it now, thanks to the efforts of the archeological services.

MACHU PICCHU

Machu Picchu was the last stronghold of Inca resistance, its citadel-refuge lost in the middle of the Andes, 7,000 feet above sea level. The city looks like a rocky spur, encircled by the deep gorges of the Rio Urubamba. The top of the spur had been leveled to make way for a central esplanade, with the various districts of the city grouped around it. The wall surrounding the city can have offered little protection against attack. The main gate where the "Way of the Inca" begins, is so poorly camouflaged that, in case of attack, it would be within a stone's throw of any assailant camped on the neighboring hill. Cultivated terraces, called *andennes,* provided the crops that fed the city. They are remarkable in many ways. For instance, these long, narrow terraces followed the mountain curves, and thus broke the slope, making it possible for land to be tilled there. They were about six feet wide and formed tiers of ribbon-like fields, some of them irrigated by water which had been channeled in. The exposure of the fields, and their altitude were varied, allowing different kinds of crops to be grown, which complemented each other.

Machu Picchu is dominated by Huayna Picchu, the summit of which can be reached by steps cut into the mountain. And even on this steep slope, open to the sky, towering above the Urubamba chasm, narrow terraces have been created.

The inhabitants of such a city were probably courageous and stubborn mountain dwellers, perhaps more preoccupied with farming every inch of available land, in one of the most hostile regions of the world, than with war and victory. A kind of challenge from humans to nature, so to speak!

CHRISTOPHER COLUMBUS

Columbus was a son of his time, a Renaissance man, and an Italian from Genoa. He was haunted by the example of two famous men, Julius Caesar and Marco Polo—Caesar, the conqueror of Gaul, and Marco Polo, who was the first European to explore China. For a long time, Columbus studied Marco Polo's travel book carefully. He was determined to reach China, but by sea instead of land. For years he searched for a sponsor who would provide him with the right ships and the right crews that would allow him to keep going farther and farther to the west.

In Spain he changed his Genoese name, Colombo, to the Spanish form, Colon, which also emphasized his desire to be a colonizer. When scholars wrote of his voyages later on, they used the Latin form—Columbus. His first name, Christopher, meant "bearer of Christ," which he felt indicated that he would bring the Christian faith to the lands he discovered.

As was the custom, Columbus drew up a plan for his intended sea voyage. He used classical writers such as Aristotle and Ptolemy, and the geographers and

monastery of La Rabida, a few miles from the seaport of Palos. Skillfully Columbus approached the King and Queen of Spain: Ferdinand of Aragon and Isabella of Castile. Commissions were set up to study his plan. But the first goal of the Catholic

monarchs was to recapture the Moorish kingdom of Granada and defeat the infidels. On January 2, 1492, Granada was taken by the Spanish army.

From then on, Ferdinand and Isabella were more willing to listen to the plan Columbus had for a transatlantic voyage. Eventually they agreed to back his voyage. On April 17, 1492, by the Capitulations of Santa Fe, Columbus was made Admiral of Castile and Viceroy of all lands discovered by him. On the morning of Friday, August 3, the great adventure began. The *Santa Maria*, escorted by the *Pinta* and the *Nina*, sailed for the open sea.

On Friday, October 12, the first new land was discovered. Guanahani was its name among the natives. The Admiral of Castile renamed it San Salvador. Today it is known as Watling Island.

December, 1492:
Columbus's travel log
I will leave here (Haiti) a number of people who are anxious, in Your Majesties' service, to discover the mine from which gold is taken . . . When I come back here, my men will have accumulated a ton of gold and spices. As a result, within three years Your Majesties will have enough money to undertake the reconquest of the Holy Sepulcher in Jerusalem. For I have always proposed that all the profits from my undertaking should be used for the liberation of Jerusalem.

Christopher Columbus
Sea Log, December 1492

mapmakers of his own time, to prove that a voyage west to the East Indies was possible. He felt so confident because he underestimated the size of the earth, and therefore the distance he would have to sail.

Columbus offered his services to Portugal, while his brother tried to raise interest in England and France. Finally, Columbus reached Spain, where he was welcomed by the Franciscan friars of the

October 12, 1492:
Columbus sets foot in the New World for the first time

At dawn, Columbus saw before him a beautiful island covered with fresh greenery and fruit trees that made it look like a huge orchard. The inhabitants came out of the woods from all sides and rushed to the shore. They were almost naked, and their gestures and behavior betrayed their profound astonishment. Columbus told his sailors to cast anchor and to equip the rowboats. He then donned a rich scarlet costume and went ashore, the royal flag of Spain in his hand.

When he landed, Columbus went down on his knees, kissed the ground, and thanked God, weeping for joy all the while. His companions followed suit. When Columbus arose, he drew his sword, unfurled the royal flag, and, on behalf of the Spanish sovereigns, took possession of the island. He called the island San Salvador. As Admiral, Viceroy, and representative of the King and Queen of Spain, he then received a pledge of allegiance from his companions.

Since Columbus believed he had landed on an island in the East Indies, he called the people he found on the island "Indians." This name was wrong, of course. Nevertheless, it not only survived but was extended to include all the native people of the New World.

J. Girardin
Life and Travels of
Christopher Columbus

Glossary

Adobe A brick made from sun-dried clay.

Agave A kind of cactus found throughout Mexico and used by the Aztecs to make cloth, in thatching, and to make *pulque*.

Altiplano The high plains found in the Andes Mountains of Peru and Bolivia. The elevation is 12,500 feet above sea-level and higher.

Andennes A flat, wide ledge cut into the mountainside by the Incas to make places where crops could be grown.

Archaeology The method of studying the past by means of excavation and examination of historical remains and ruins.

Assagai A thin spear or javelin made from wood.

Atlantes A supporting column sculpted in the figure of a man.

Bark A small sailing ship.

Calmecac A boarding school where Aztec boys were trained to be priests.

Causeway A raised road or pathway built across marshy land or low water.

Cenote A deep sinkhole with a pool at the bottom.

Chinampa An island built by the Aztecs out of layers of reeds, other plants, and mud and planted with crops.

Codex Old Aztec manuscript in which history and religious teachings were recorded.

Conquistador A Spanish conqueror in North or South America during the 1500s.

Coracle A basket-like boat made with a wooden frame covered with wicker and waterproofed with pitch or animal skin.

Eldorado The legendary city of great riches sought by the Spanish explorers in America.

Equinox Either of the two times (March 21 and September 22) of the year when, because of the position of the sun, day and night are of equal length in all parts of the world.

Fresco A picture that has been painted on a wall or ceiling before the plaster has dried.

Glacier A slow-moving, large body of ice.

Glyph A small picture used for writing instead of words.

Irrigate To bring water to crops usually through canals, ditches, or pipes.

Isthmus A narrow strip of land connecting two larger bodies of land.

Jade A green colored semi-precious stone which was much prized by the Aztecs.

Megalith A huge stone used in ancient construction.

Monolith A monumemt or statue made from a single large block of stone.

Necropolis A burial ground dating back to ancient or prehistoric times.

Obsidian Volcanic glass used to make spearheads and blades.

Palanquin A method of transportation for one person that is made up of an enclosed couch and is carried on the shoulders of several men by means of poles.

Plateau A large, high quite flat area that is raised above the surrounding land.

Pre-Columbian Having to do with the time before Columbus came to the Americas.

Rhizome A root-like stem that grows underground.

Solstice One of two times during the year when the sun is at its greatest distance from the equator. In the Northern Hemisphere the summer solstice is the longest day of the year and the winter solstice the shortest.

Stela (pl. **stelae**) An upright slab or pillar of stone on which there is some kind of design or inscription.

Strait A narrow body of water that connects two larger bodies of water.

Telpochcalli The school where Aztec boys were trained as warriors.

Tlaloc The Rain God.

Tortilla A thin, flat, round cake made from corn.

Tuff A rock made from volcanic ash and other erupted material.

Index

1 2 3 4 5 6 7 8 9 10—U—93 92 91 90 89 88 87 86 85